THE
DECISION-MAKER'S
GUIDE TO
LONG-TERM
FINANCING

The Essential Handbook on Securing Financing Terms with Confidence

Kathrin Ohle

twig energy inc.

Library and Archives Canada Cataloguing in Publication

Ohle, Kathrin, 1965-, author
   The decision-maker's guide to long-term financing : the essential handbook on
securing financing terms with confidence / Kathrin Ohle.

Includes bibliographical references and index.
Issued in print and electronic formats.
ISBN 978-0-9936840-0-5 (pbk.).—ISBN 978-0-9936840-1-2 (epub).—
ISBN 978-0-9936840-2-9 (mobi).—ISBN 978-0-9936840-3-6 (pdf)

1. Long-term business financing—Handbooks, manuals, etc.
2. Business enterprises—Finance—Handbooks, manuals, etc. I. Title.

HG4027.3.O34 2014   658.15   C2014-900789-2
                                           C2014-900790-6

Design and production: Kevin Cockburn/PageWave Graphics Inc.
Editor: Sue Sumeraj
Proofreader: Wendy Potter
Indexer: Gillian Watts

The inspiring quote on page 3 is from Marianne Williamson's book *A Return
to Love: Reflections on the Principles of a Course in Miracles* (New York:
HarperCollins, 1992), pages 190–191. Used with permission.

. . . .

Our deepest fear is not that we are inadequate.
Our deepest fear is that we are powerful beyond measure.
It is our light, not our darkness that most frightens us.
We ask ourselves, Who am I to be brilliant,
gorgeous, talented, fabulous?
Actually, who are you not to be? You are a child of God.
Your playing small does not serve the world.
There is nothing enlightened about shrinking so that
other people won't feel insecure around you.
We are all meant to shine, as children do.
We were born to make manifest
the glory of God that is within us.
It's not just in some of us; it's in everyone.
And as we let our own light shine,
we unconsciously give other people permission
to do the same.
As we are liberated from our own fear, our presence
automatically liberates others.

— Marianne Williamson

CONTENTS

Chapter Three: Debt Financing   45

Chapter Four: Subordinate Financing 79

Chapter Five: The Mechanics of a Financing Transaction 87

Introduction

During my more than 20 years of investing and lending, I have spoken with countless entrepreneurs and businesspeople within small and medium-sized enterprises who regularly make financing decisions without having a financing background. Because of this experience, and because every business decision is essentially a financing decision, I felt compelled to create a practical, comprehensive textbook that addresses the typical financing topics such decision-makers are frequently exposed to.

This book is for all entrepreneurs and businesspeople in small to medium-sized companies who are part of the company's management team and who, correspondingly, make or influence company decisions. The information in this book will help save your company time and money, and it will help you secure the most beneficial and suitable terms and conditions for your long-term financing transactions.

Who Should Read This Book?

This book is written for the decision-makers in any type of business, especially those who do not have an extensive financing background. As all business decisions are essentially financing decisions, this book targets anyone on the management team. Investors and lenders will investigate all parts of a business — management, sales and marketing, operations, purchasing and personnel. They will also review the expertise of all people on the management team. Consequently, any major decision in any part of the business has an impact on the company's ability to attract financing.

I am passionate about helping you make well-informed decisions, be successful and grow your company and, as a result, have a positive impact on the economy, other people and the planet. Based on my experience, I know this book will help you achieve success. As I wrote, I put myself in your shoes, anticipating what type of questions you might have and what information you might need. Consequently, I am confident that you will find answers to your most pressing financing questions here.

There are thousands of books on financing available worldwide, but to my knowledge, none of them outlines in a concise and informative way all the relevant long-term financing decisions a businessperson faces on a regular basis.

This book focuses on conveying a solid base knowledge of long-term financing via equity, debt and subordinate financing — the forms of long-term financing that entrepreneurs or the management teams of small to medium-sized companies will typically seek out at some point during their start-up and growth phases. It also runs through the mechanics of a financing transaction, to help your company achieve its financing goals. It does not dissect structures like working capital financing or letter of credit financing, nor does it address cross-border financing, government financing through avenues such as grant programs, loan guarantees or tax and other incentives, or the types of financing that are only available for amounts greater than $50 million to $100 million, like bond financings or securitizations. It also does not cover emerging types of financing, such as crowdfunding or community bonds. Those topics are for another book.

While offering definitions of the terms used, the book also brings them to life by putting them in the context of examples from real-world situations I come across frequently. Given that my financial advisory firm focuses on the clean technology and alternative energy sectors, many of the examples I use are taken from those areas. However, the information provided applies across most industries, and the examples are intended to show potential solutions to problems your company may be encountering.

How you use this book is up to you: you can read it from cover to cover, or you can use the comprehensive table of contents and expansive index to locate specific sections that are of interest to you at a given time.

Wishing you much success!

With warmth,
Kathrin Ohle

GLOSSARY OF ACRONYMS AND INITIALISMS

COD	Commercial operation date
CPC	Capital pool company
DSCR	Debt service coverage ratio
DSRA	Debt service reserve account
EBITDA	Earnings before interest, taxes, depreciation and amortization
EPC	Engineering, procurement and construction
EPCM	Engineering, procurement and construction management
EPS	Earnings per share
GSA	General security agreement
ICR	Interest coverage ratio
IP	Intellectual property
IPO	Initial public offering
IRR	Internal rate of return
LIBOR	London Interbank Offered Rate
LLCR	Loan life coverage ratio
LOI	Letter of intent
MAC	Material adverse change
MMRA	Major maintenance reserve account
MOU	Memorandum of understanding
n/a	Not applicable
NPV	Net present value
O&M	Operations and maintenance
RAROC	Risk-adjusted return on capital
ROFO	Right of first offer
ROFR	Right of first refusal
RTO	Reverse takeover
SPAC	Special purpose acquisition corporation
TSX	Toronto Stock Exchange
WACC	Weighted average cost of capital

CHAPTER ONE

SETTING
THE STAGE

A Dream Fulfilled

Matteo had always dreamed of acquiring his own printing business, and finally felt like he was ready to achieve that goal. He did his research and found the company he wanted to buy: a business that had been founded decades ago and enjoyed solid profits. He negotiated a purchase price of $2.4 million, of which he was able to contribute $400,000 of his own money (that is, his equity contribution). So he was faced with a financing gap of $2.0 million, which he needed to raise from other sources.

He first approached various banks in an attempt to borrow the money he needed through traditional debt financing — a loan, in other words. Matteo was pleased with the company's fixed assets, consisting of machines and other equipment, which were well maintained and capable of satisfying immediate growth demands. He believed he could continue operating the business for the foreseeable future with no need for any material capital expenditures. The banks took a contrary view, however; they didn't assign the assets much value, as they were largely depreciated, and therefore deemed them unacceptable as collateral. Matteo was disappointed that he was able to attract only $100,000 in traditional debt financing (also known as senior debt financing), but his bank of choice also provided a line of credit against the company's accounts receivable and inventory.

Since he was still substantially short of the amount he needed to purchase the company, Matteo decided to look into subordinate financing. Based on the company's solid cash flow, he was able to secure $800,000 in subordinate financing. The same financial institution also provided $400,000 of equity (institutional equity). Matteo then negotiated a financing arrangement of $600,000 with the current owner of the company (vendor financing). The final $100,000 came from a friend in the form of a convertible debenture.

The table at the top of page 13 provides a summary of Matteo's purchase transaction.

Matteo's example demonstrates how various financing instruments can come together to produce a beneficial outcome — the realization of a person's dream. The various financing instruments touched on here will be discussed in greater detail throughout this book.

Events that Trigger the Need for Financing

When does the need for long-term financing arise? One possibility is the acquisition of company shares (as in Matteo's case), assets or a group of assets. Two other key events that trigger the need for financing are the start-up of a new business and the expansion of an existing, growing business.

USES OF THE FUNDS			SOURCES OF THE FUNDS		
Share Purchase	$2,400,000	100%	Matteo's Equity	$400,000	17%
			Senior Debt Financing	$100,000	4%
			Subordinate Financing	$800,000	33%
			Institutional Equity	$400,000	17%
			Vendor Financing	$600,000	25%
			Convertible Debenture	$100,000	4%
TOTAL	**$2,400,000**	**100%**	**TOTAL**	**$2,400,000**	**100%**

The Balance Sheet

In financing, it all starts with the balance sheet, the framework through which financing activities are reflected. A balance sheet lists, as of a certain date, a company's assets, liabilities and equity. The difference between the company's assets and liabilities is known as equity, capital, net assets or net worth.

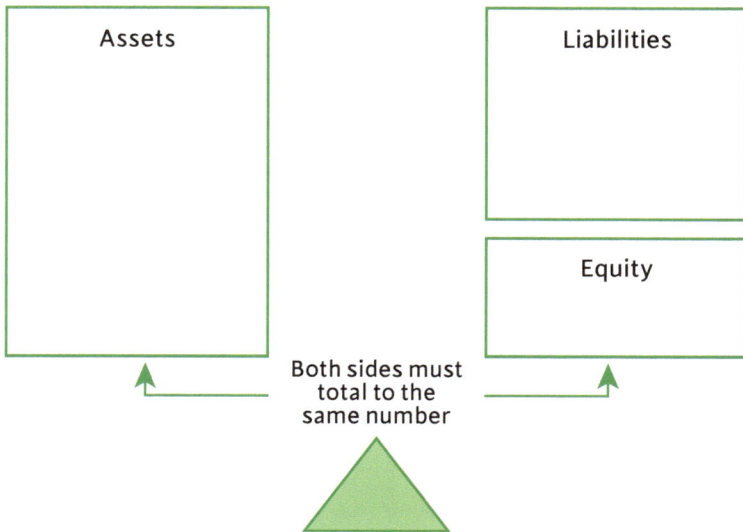

FIGURE 1: THE BALANCE SHEET

Assets are listed on the left side of the balance sheet, while liabilities plus equity make up the right side. Both sides amount to the same value or, in other words, are in balance. The asset side of the balance sheet shows what the company's money has been spent on ("uses"). The right side illustrates where the money came from — how the assets have been financed ("sources"), either through liabilities or from equity. The table at the top of page 13 is an example of a balance sheet.

When the company raises equity or takes on debt, the balance sheet extends. In other words, the company adds dollars to the right side of the balance sheet (extending its equity or its liabilities, respectively). Correspondingly, the asset side of the balance sheet extends as well, as the company either purchases assets with the money raised or parks the money in a bank account.

> ▶ **DEFINITION**
>
> **Financing:** The provision of funds or capital for investment or the acquisition of assets.

The Main Types of Financing

This book explains how to meet your company's needs through equity financing, debt financing and/or subordinate financing. A company can attract equity financing at any stage of its development, though the type of investor will differ depending on the stage, as outlined in Stages of Equity Financing (page 19). To qualify for debt financing, the company must be more mature, demonstrating stability and having experienced typically three years of solid financial performance in terms of revenues, cash flow and net income. To attract subordinate financing, the company must be cash-flow positive and must generate sufficient cash flow to justify this type of loan.

Equity Financing

In equity financing, an investor provides funds in exchange for shares of the company (ownership shares). Details on equity financing are found in Chapter Two, including:

- its characteristics as expressed through ranking and return;
- the type of equity investors that are available during specific stages of a company's development;
- a comparison of strategic investors to financial investors;
- the equity-raising alternatives: private placement vs. public offering;

- the key terms of a shareholder agreement, with an emphasis on the possible pitfalls; and
- methods of valuation.

Debt Financing

In debt financing, the company borrows money from lenders against a promise to pay interest and repay the principal. Details on debt financing are found in Chapter Three, including:

- the difference between recourse and non-recourse financing;
- types of lenders and loans;
- project financing (without recourse) vs. corporate financing (with recourse);
- key criteria that need to be fulfilled to attract the desired financing;
- loan syndication, where a loan is provided by a group of lenders; and
- financial leases.

Subordinate Financing

Subordinate financing is a form of debt financing with equity-like characteristics. Details on subordinate financing are found in Chapter Four, including:

- the characteristics and benefits of this financing instrument;
- the difference between "sub debt" and "mezzanine debt";
- the terms and conditions of the loan agreement;
- the main criteria of the subordination and postponement agreement;
- convertible debentures; and
- vendor financing.

Achieving Your Goals

The final chapter of the book pulls together all the mechanics of a financing transaction, to help your company achieve its financing goals. In Chapter Five, you will find information on:

- how to decide which types of financing to pursue;
- the due diligence investigation;
- return calculations and expectations;
- making your pitch; and
- the investing and lending processes.

CHAPTER 2

EQUITY FINANCING

What Is Equity Financing?

Equity, in simple terms, is the interest an investor has in an asset or business after deduction of all liabilities. Since this book examines equity within the context of a business, equity financing is the act of raising funds through the sale of company shares (also called stock). In other words, an investor pays money for company shares, which represent a portion of ownership of that company.

Raising equity takes perseverance and optimism. As you go through the process of equity financing, keep in mind that by selling equity you will be responsible for administering somebody else's money — somebody who does not know you, your technology or your markets as well as you do, but who has very real expectations of enjoying financial returns from your efforts.

Common Shares versus Preferred Shares

Most companies are established with simple common share structures, but company ownership can also come in the form of preferred shares. Common shares are the basic option, giving the owner the rights outlined in the company's articles of incorporation and bylaws, and in its shareholder agreement as applicable. Common shareholders have voting rights and thus the opportunity to control the direction of the company. Common shares are generally held by founders and employees.

> ▶ **DEFINITION**
>
> **Dividend:** The portion of the net profit that is paid to the owners (shareholders) of a business. A fixed dividend is a set amount per share.

While common shares do not have a fixed dividend attached to them, preferred shares usually do. However, a company does not have to pay a fixed dividend if it lacks the funds to do so. Preferred shares also have associated rights that differentiate them from common shares. These rights vary substantially: Preferred shareholders can be voting or non-voting, may hold security rights against specific assets, and may even have special voting rights with respect to election of directors or certain extraordinary events, such as issuance of new shares or the acquisition of another company. They may also possess more extensive dilution protection provisions than common shares, and other provisions may be created to address specific tax or ownership structuring issues. Furthermore, preferred shares rank higher than common shares in the ownership structure of the company. Preferred shares are generally held by financial investors.

Ranking of Shares

An equity investor ranks below (or is junior to) all of the company's creditors. Within the group of equity investors, however, a ranking can be structured through different classes of shares. Preferred shares typically have a certain dividend percentage attached to them. They also rank above (or are senior to) common shares. Further differentiation in dividends and ranking can be made through different classes of preferred shares: preferred A, B, C, and so on. Only when all preferred shareholders have received their dividends will the common shareholder be paid a dividend, assuming further distributable earnings are available. In the case of bankruptcy, once the company's creditors have been paid off, any remaining assets are distributed to the holders of the preferred stock before common shareholders receive anything.

TYPE OF EQUITY	RANKING	RECEIVES DIVIDENDS
Common shares	Junior to preferred shares	Yes, subordinated to preferred shares and the company's creditors
Preferred shares	Senior to common shares	Yes, subordinated to the company's creditors

FIGURE 2: COMMON SHARES VERSUS PREFERRED SHARES

Return Expectations

The lower the ranking of the investor, the higher the risks and the financier's return expectations. Common shares do not have a fixed dividend attached to them, and they are subordinated to all preferred shares and the company's creditors. Correspondingly, the common shares' return is uncertain. They have the highest risk. To compensate for that risk, investors will only be enticed to invest in common shares if they believe the shares will generate a certain return over time. Their return expectation will be higher than that of preferred shareholders, whose return expectation will be higher than that of lenders.

Stages of Equity Financing

Sources of capital tend to evolve through the following stages, in line with the maturity of the company requiring the funds.

▶ **DEFINITION**

Capital: Cash or other assets used to generate an income — a return — through investment in a business.

Seed Capital

Seed capital is usually provided at start-up by the founders of the company, in the form of cash and/or sweat equity. Sweat equity refers to equity ownership acquired through work put into a company without the payment of cash — an investment of time for equity.

Friends, Family and Angel Investors

Should the founders require more money to support the company, they may be able to raise funds from friends, family and angel investors. Government grant programs may also be available at this stage or a later one. The benefit of government grants is that they typically do not require the company to give up ownership and, therefore, do not dilute the ownership. That said, some government programs have a "repayable" component where a portion of the grant must be repaid to the government within a certain period of time, possibly with interest.

> ▶ **DEFINITION**
>
> **Angel Investor:** An individual who provides equity at an early stage of a company's development, when the risk is high. An angel investor typically invests after friends and family, but before venture capital funds would make an investment.

Preferred Series A Stock Financing

This type of financing is also called the "A" round. It is usually provided by angels and venture capital funds, and sometimes by strategic investors. By this stage, the company's product development is advanced, but the company is still burning cash (that is, its expenses still exceed its revenues, if any). It may still be years until the company is profitable. Further venture capital rounds may follow.

> ▶ **DEFINITION**
>
> **Venture Capital:** Funds provided to early-stage, high-risk businesses with substantial upside potential.

Growth Capital

At this stage, the company has a track record, or history, of sales growth, generating material and increasing revenues. The company may not yet be profitable, but it is evolving towards sustained profitability. Once profitable, the company will have to reinvest its profits to feed its growth. It will also require additional capital to finance expansion into new markets or new product lines, and to cover associated capital expenditures and working capital needs. Sources of growth capital include private equity funds (more so than venture capital funds), strategic investors and the public markets (through a public offering of shares). Once the company is cash-flow positive, institutional lenders (such as banks, pension funds and life insurance companies) will become an option for debt financing.

Private equity funds are in the business of making direct investments in later-stage, more mature companies, typically with focus on the growth of the company or to assist in buying out current shareholders. They usually invest in private companies, not in publicly traded entities. The money the fund invests is typically raised from institutional and accredited investors. The fund commonly generates a financial return on the money invested on "exit," when it sells its shares in the investee company for a capital gain. It may also receive dividend income along the way.

Venture capital funds usually invest in earlier-stage, higher-risk businesses with substantial upside potential. The money the fund invests can come from all types of sources, such as institutional or retail (i.e., individual) investors, strategic investors or foundations. Like private equity funds, a venture capital fund typically generates a financial return on the capital invested at exit, when it sells its shares in the investee company for a capital gain.

Strategic Investors versus Financial Investors

In the context of this book, a strategic investor is a company that is active in the same industry as the business looking for money, or a complementary one. A strategic investor has the potential to bring more to the table than just capital, particularly access to accelerated growth in revenues, a sense of mentorship and a network along the value chain. A financial investor is one whose business it is to make money from investing money; this type of investor is simply looking for a financial return.

> ▶ **DEFINITION**
>
> **Value Chain:** The value creation process for a product or service, from raw materials to sales, with value increasing along the way. For example, activities on the value chain could include growing, harvesting, refining feedstock, manufacturing of raw materials, supply of raw materials, manufacturing of final products, marketing and sales, to name a few.

Return requirements go hand in hand with the perceived risk: the higher the perceived risk, the higher the return expectation. Strategic investors will often be satisfied with a lower return than financial investors because they are familiar with the business and have the expertise to step in and operate it; they may therefore perceive the risk as being lower than a financial investor would. Strategic investors may also accept lower returns because they believe the business will provide other benefits in the form of synergies or future business opportunities.

Financial investors will frequently have to rely on independent consultants to assess at least some of the risk, especially technology risk, and it will often take them longer to get comfortable with the risk. Strategic investors will be able to assess the risk and complete their due diligence investigation more promptly through in-house experts and, hence, make decisions faster. Should, however, the strategic investor be a large organization, the decision process may be slowed down by the wait for scheduled investment committee and/or board meetings or to convene extraordinary investment committee/board meetings.

There are also some specific challenges to consider when it comes to strategic investors. Publicly traded strategic investors, for example, may only make investments that increase (or are accretive to) their earnings per share either right away or within a short period of time. Furthermore, strategic investors may ask for a right of first refusal (ROFR) with respect to certain rights, projects or products, which gives them the option to purchase such rights, projects or products at the price and terms set out in a third-party offer. The trouble with giving an investor a ROFR is that any prospective third-party buyers, knowing about this right, may be reluctant to enter into serious negotiations with the company, as they may fear being used just to establish a price between the company and the person holding the ROFR. This may lead the prospective third-party buyers to offer a lower price for the rights, projects or products, which, in turn, will also reduce the company's negotiation power with the holder of the ROFR. (See also "Right of First Refusal," page 32.)

> ▶ **DEFINITION**
>
> **Lead Investor:** The investor during a financing round who is the first to make a commitment. This is usually an investor who has a very good understanding of the risks; other investors generally find comfort in the lead investor's vote of confidence and jump in on the investment.

Financial investors may be more motivated to invest once a lead investor is established. This can be, and often is, a cumbersome process. Financial investors tend to receive a lot of requests, so putting effort into a warm call and understanding their investment criteria is crucial. Should you be searching for venture capital money, keep the following in mind: If you are sparsely funded, it will be hard to compete on the world stage with companies that are better funded. So you may have to look globally, where funds have raised larger amounts of money. Larger funds with larger portfolios are able to provide larger amounts of money (for the initial fundraising round as well as for follow-on rounds). They also have domain experts, giving the transaction a chance of going through a predictable investment process instead of a potentially drawn-out education process.

> ▶ **DEFINITION**
>
> **Warm Call:** Making contact based on a previous interaction or a third-party referral, as opposed to a cold call, where there is no known connection between the prospect and the caller.

Both strategic investors and financial investors almost always require the founders of the company to have "skin in the game," meaning that the founders have cash invested — enough to hurt should they lose it. Sweat equity is usually heavily discounted or may not even qualify at all, as it is considered sunk capital. Investors believe that putting real money into an endeavour motivates founders to do anything to ensure its success. There is no hard number for what the appropriate investment amount is, but it should be a material investment in relation to the founders' personal net worth. When both founders and investors have money at risk, they are what is often called "aligned," as the interests of the company's management and those of its investors are in synch. Both parties are focused on generating a financial return on the invested capital.

Frequently, either type of investor will want to secure a seat on the company's board or, at a minimum, an observer role at board meetings to ensure information flow and some control. Furthermore, financial investors tend to strive for a substantial minority of shares. The ownership stake a strategic investor prefers depends on the specific situation.

A strategic investor's expertise and reputation may play an instrumental role in securing debt financing for the company, giving lenders added comfort. Strategic investors may also be prepared to get directly involved in debt financing by providing a loan themselves or guaranteeing one, thereby solving short-term bridging needs or affording longer-term solutions. In contrast, with a financial investor, the company will commonly have to rely on its own merits to secure additional funding. However, a financial investor may be helpful in structuring the debt transaction and in bringing lenders to the table.

With respect to the exit strategy, strategic investors are more likely to take a long-term view, while financial investors often have a specific time frame for a financial return in mind, generally within three to five years. That said, if the investment is in an infrastructure asset with predictable long-term returns, certain financial investors (such as infrastructure funds, pension funds or life insurance companies) may have the mandate to keep the investment for the long haul and enjoy the annuity-like returns.

Some of the added benefits — or value-adds — a strategic investor may bring to the table are expertise in development, deployment of technology, and operations and management (O&M). Furthermore, a strategic investor may provide a recognized name and a solid reputation, instrumental support in proving a concept, and helpful contacts along the value chain. Financial investors, due to their exposure to various sectors, possibly worldwide, may have very helpful contacts.

	STRATEGIC INVESTORS	FINANCIAL INVESTORS
Return requirements/ perceived risk	Lower	Higher
Evaluation of risk	Have the experts in-house to evaluate the risk; will be more comfortable with the risk, as it is within their expertise; could more easily step in	Will need more convincing to get comfortable with the risk
Due diligence	Will likely be able to assess technology risk on their own	Will need to hire independent consultants to assess technology risk
Specific challenges	A publicly traded strategic investor may have additional hurdles, such as EPS accretion; issue of ROFR	Potential requirement of a lead investor, warm calls, a global view
Skin in the game	Important	Important
Governance/ control	Board seat for control and information	Board seat for control and information
Debt financing	Creditworthiness will positively impact debt financing; may provide (interim) debt financing from their own balance sheet, or guarantees	May be helpful in bringing lenders to the table and structuring the debt transaction
Exit strategy	Longer-term view	Very important (usually 3 to 5 years)
Value-adds	Expertise in development, deployment, O&M; name/reputation; support in proof of concept; contacts	Contacts
Transaction needs to be ...	LOGICAL	ECONOMICAL ("A DEAL")

FIGURE 3: STRATEGIC INVESTORS VERSUS FINANCIAL INVESTORS

▶ **DEFINITION**

Proof of Concept: A demonstration that a chosen method is feasible. This test is usually conducted on a much smaller scale than the method the business plans on implementing once it is proven.

In conclusion, strategic investors will pursue transactions that make logical sense, first and foremost, while financial investors will be motivated by transactions that make economic sense.

Private Placement versus Public Offering

When it comes to selling, or "raising," equity, there are numerous paths companies can take to achieve success. However, they typically fall into two broad categories: selling equity privately (private placement) or offering equity in the public markets (public offering). A private placement is often associated with companies that are, as defined, private (not publicly traded). A public offering is carried out by a company that is either going public and raising equity (by selling a percentage of the company) or that is already publicly traded and is issuing more shares to raise equity (often called a secondary offering).

Whenever a company makes an offering of common or preferred shares to the public, it is obliged to register the issue with the relevant securities commission. This is a costly undertaking that can be avoided by selling the securities privately. A disadvantage of private placement is the lack of liquidity: securities can be more easily resold in public markets than in private ones.

> ▶ **DEFINITION**
>
> **Security:** A financial instrument that is tradable and entitles the holder to certain rights, such as ownership, payment of principal and interest, or purchase of shares. Securities include shares, bonds, debentures and options.

Private Placement

In a private placement, the security is negotiated directly between the company and the investor(s), often with the help of a financial advisor. Consequently, the security can be tailored for companies with specific opportunities or issues. Renegotiations in response to unexpected circumstances are extremely cumbersome for public issues but manageable for private placements. The relationship between the parties of a private placement is more intimate. However, the advantages of the closer relationship, with tailored agreements, also cost money. The investors will want to be compensated for their own due diligence investigation to understand the risks, as well as for the lack of liquidity.

Public Offering

Going public is as much a philosophy as it is a way of raising equity. Running a publicly traded company is very different from running a private company. You are continuously in the public eye, speaking frequently to your company's financial performance, business plan and milestones. Business decisions will have to be made along the lines of the proclaimed business strategy, to document consistency. Financial reporting and controls, as well as corporate governance, will

	PRIVATE PLACEMENT	PUBLIC OFFERING
Contracts	Customized	Not customized
Renegotiations	Manageable	Extremely cumbersome
Investor relationship	More intimate	Less intimate, or anonymous
Due diligence investigation	Investors will have to perform their own and determine risks	Prospectus provides necessary information and spells out risks
Liquidity	Less liquid than public offering	More liquid than private placement
Cost	Less costly than public offering	More costly than private placement

FIGURE 4: PRIVATE PLACEMENT VERSUS PUBLIC OFFERING

need to be at a standard suitable for a public company. In summary, a public company deals with loss of control and confidentiality, initial and ongoing expenses, periodic reporting requirements and shareholder expectations.

INSIDER TIP ▶ Going public is as much a philosophy as it is a way of raising funds.

Before letting the issues of going and being public dissuade you, however, weigh them against the attractive benefits. Being public provides the company with broader access to capital and future financing opportunities — from expansion of operations to acquisitions. The issuance of shares to the public expands the company's investor base, affords a continual (and, once public, cost-effective) form of valuation and helps set the stage for future secondary equity financings (facilitating access to capital). Financial institutions may also concede more favourable lending terms to a public company than to a private one. Because of disclosure requirements and the highly regulated environment, available information on the public company tends to be more standardized and complete than what is voluntarily provided by a private company. Generally, this gives lenders a higher comfort level.

Public companies are also required to have a high level of discipline, an obligation that can often prove quite valuable. A highly disciplined environment driven by financial performance can help rapidly growing companies transition from the "entrepreneurial phase" to a more mature phase.

A public company is able to use its shares instead of cash to acquire other companies, an approach that may allow for a more timely and cost-effective completion of mergers and acquisitions. Furthermore, financing an acquisition through shares may be more tax-efficient. For example, in many tax jurisdictions, shareholders exchanging their private company shares for public company shares may be eligible for tax relief from capital gains until the publicly traded shares are sold — a selling feature for target companies.

Going public not only increases the company's visibility, it creates a permanent public eye on the company. The public filing of documents, equity research analysis and media coverage enhance public awareness and, generally, result in a higher profile and greater credibility for the company. In consequence, a broader, more diversified group of investors becomes available, the demand for the company's shares grows, and the value to the company's shareholders increases.

Unlike a private company, a public company can participate in a stock market, a regulated vehicle where its shares can be traded publicly and efficiently. This increases the liquidity of the company shares dramatically, which, in turn, should lead to a higher valuation.

Being public also benefits both the employers and employees of the company: Stock options and employee share purchase plans are an alternative way of compensating employees, allowing employees to participate in the ownership of the company and benefit from being shareholders, while having a lower impact on the employer's cash flow. These plans tie employees' compensation to the company's performance and, thereby, strengthen employees' commitment to the company. Stock options can also be used as a recruitment incentive. This said, stock options and employee share purchase plans may have an adverse impact on the employee tax treatment and should therefore be considered very carefully in advance.

The main advantages and disadvantages of going public are summarized in Figure 5.

ADVANTAGES	DISADVANTAGES
Broader access to capital	Public exposure, disclosure, accountability
Company valuation on a continual and cost-effective basis	Loss of control and confidentiality
Liquidity for shareholders	Periodic reporting at a high standard
Enhanced credibility	Initial and ongoing expenses
Required discipline assists companies in transition	
Shares can be used as a currency substitute	
Shares can be used as employee compensation tools	

FIGURE 5: MAIN ADVANTAGES AND DISADVANTAGES OF GOING PUBLIC

Going Public

There are various ways of listing on a stock exchange, and they differ from exchange to exchange and from country to country. Many stock exchanges also run junior exchanges, which act as an incubator and allow smaller and less mature companies to list. Junior exchanges often have much lower listing requirements than their senior counterparts. Companies traded on a junior exchange tend to be riskier investments than the ones traded on the senior exchange. Some exchanges also operate "junior junior exchanges," which are incubators for junior exchanges, allowing companies to list under even more relaxed requirements. Furthermore, some exchanges offer "blind pool" programs, unique listing vehicles that raise money without specifying what it will be used for (see page 30 for more information on blind pools).

Figure 6 lists some of the largest stock exchanges. It is not intended to be a comprehensive list, but rather has been compiled to give the reader a flavour of the most prominent stock exchanges around the world. Examples of junior and junior junior exchanges are: BATS Z-Exchange and BATS Y-Exchange in the United States; TSX Venture Exchange and Canadian National Stock Exchange in Canada; and Growth Enterprise Market in Hong Kong.

COUNTRY	STOCK EXCHANGE
North America	
Canada	Toronto Stock Exchange
United States	NYSE Euronext (USA) NASDAQ OMX
South America	
Brazil	BM&F Bovespa
Europe	**NYSE Euronext (Europe)**
Germany	Deutsche Boerse
Russia	Moscow Exchange
Spain	BME Spanish Exchange
Switzerland	SIX Swiss Exchange
United Kingdom	London Stock Exchange
Asia	
China	Shanghai Stock Exchange Shenzhen Stock Exchange
Hong Kong	Hong Kong Stock Exchange

COUNTRY	STOCK EXCHANGE
India	Bombay Stock Exchange National Stock Exchange of India
Japan	Tokyo Stock Exchange
Singapore	Singapore Exchange
South Korea	Korea Exchange
Taiwan	Taiwan Stock Exchange
Australia	
Australia	Australian Securities Exchange
Africa	
South Africa	Johannesburg Stock Exchange

FIGURE 6: OVERVIEW OF SOME OF THE LARGEST EXCHANGES IN THE WORLD

Source: World Federation of Exchanges; twig energy inc.

If you are considering going public, you will definitely want to get input from expert advisors on the best way to do so. In principle, there are two ways for small to medium-sized companies to access publicly traded markets: the traditional way (an initial public offering) or an alternative method.

Initial Public Offering

An initial public offering (IPO) is a relatively straightforward way to go public. The business prepares a detailed prospectus, files it with the relevant securities commission and stock exchange and, upon acceptance of the prospectus by the regulatory authorities, completes an application for a public listing with the applicable stock exchange.

The prospectus outlines the investment offering in detail, including all possible opportunities and risks, to provide potential investors with the information they require to make an informed decision. Because the prospectus is a crucial part of the application process, the company's management team, financial advisors, auditors and legal counsel, as well as advisors from the stock exchange and securities commission, will work together to create this document.

An IPO is a good choice for a pre-existing, disciplined business that can systematically prepare itself to go through the public offering process. Aside from the backing of the company's board of directors, the support of an appropriate investment community sponsor is likely the most critical requirement for a successful IPO. With the right sponsorship, the process of going public can be a very pleasant experience.

You can acquire a significant amount of helpful information on the IPO process simply by approaching the stock exchange you are interested in listing on.

Their business is listing and trading shares; you are their potential client, so they will be happy to assist you and answer your questions.

Alternative Ways to Go Public

There are several alternative ways for a private company to go public, most of which involve some form of transaction (such as a merger or reverse takeover) with a pre-existing publicly traded company.

Merger

In a merger (also known as a plan of arrangement or a scheme of arrangement), the company wanting to go public merges with one that is already listed and whose business activities appear to be a good fit. The private company effectively surrenders all its shares for shares of the public company. The percentage that the selling shareholders will own of the publicly traded company varies with each transaction. The parties enter into a definitive merger agreement and obtain approval from the shareholders and the regulatory authorities.

Reverse Takeover

In a reverse takeover (RTO), the company looking to go public is taken over by (or sold to) a pre-existing business that is already listed and that often has no substantial business activity. Generally, such a listed business has failed and its public vehicle is now seeking an alternative business for the listed "shell." A defining feature of an RTO is that the company being taken over typically takes control of a majority of the shares of the listed company after the takeover. An RTO requires considerable financial and technical expertise, as the listed shell often has legacy issues, such as environmental liabilities, and/or assets that may be irrelevant or, worse, burdensome or confusing to investors.

Blind Pool

Many jurisdictions permit the creation of a "blind pool" of capital, which raises money from investors without supplying any information on how the funds will be used. Obviously, this is a higher-risk transaction for the investor.

In Canada, a blind pool can be created through the capital pool company (CPC) program offered by the TSX Venture Exchange. A CPC is a shell company, typically with modest capital. The CPC and its advisors will create a prospectus to raise money for the identification and evaluation of potential acquisitions — again, without specifying an acquisition candidate. The CPC then files the prospectus with the relevant provincial securities commission(s) and applies for listing on the TSX Venture Exchange. Upon regulatory approval and completion of the distribution of shares (or the fundraising), the CPC starts trading with ".P" at the end of its ticker symbol.

Once listed, the CPC has 24 months to identify a target as its qualifying transaction. The TSX Venture Exchange will then evaluate whether the target company meets minimum listing requirements. Upon the exchange's confirmation, the CPC will complete the acquisition. The CPC then trades as a regular TSX Venture–listed company, with the ".P" removed from the ticker symbol.

In the United States, a blind pool can be established through the special purpose acquisition corporation (SPAC) program offered by the New York Stock Exchange and NASDAQ. Unlike a traditional IPO, the SPAC program enables seasoned directors and officers to form a corporation that contains no commercial operations or assets other than cash. The SPAC is then listed on the exchange via an IPO. Ninety percent of the funds raised in the IPO are placed in escrow, to be used towards a future acquisition. Within 24 months of the SPAC's listing, it must complete a qualifying acquisition of a business or asset. Assuming the acquisition meets the exchange's listing requirements, the SPAC's shares will continue trading as a regular listing.

For a wealth of information on the various alternatives in your jurisdiction, visit the website of the World Exchange Federation (http://www.world-exchanges.org/member-exchanges/key-information) and link to the website of your relevant stock exchange.

The Shareholder Agreement: Selected Key Terms

The shareholder agreement stipulates the terms the shareholders of a corporation must agree to, essentially laying out the benefits and risks of ownership. It covers such topics as governance and control (e.g., voting rights, size and composition of the board of directors, quorum requirements, frequency of board meetings), covenants (e.g., regarding the provision of certain information), transfer of shares, funding arrangements (e.g., to prevent dilution), termination, dispute resolution and confidentiality. Shareholder agreements can range from very simple to very complex.

A company is not legally required to put a shareholder agreement in place; it can simply be governed by its statutes alone, along with its articles of incorporation and bylaws. However, the company's statutes, articles of incorporation and bylaws will not address the diverging interests of minority and majority shareholders, or founding partners and investor-type shareholders. Accordingly, even in smaller companies, shareholders tend to enter into shareholder agreements.

Without construing any legal advice or opinion, the following are the main terms that require negotiation and have a major impact on the shareholder's risks and benefits. This is not an exhaustive list of key items to be considered when negotiating a shareholder agreement. Rather, it is intended to illustrate the complex issues and interests that must be addressed when documenting the rights and obligations of shareholders. As most of these items will be raised during the "term sheet" stage of negotiations, it is important to involve legal counsel early on in the process.

Transfer of Shares

A shareholder agreement will generally be structured to prohibit the transfer of shares, to protect against unknown or unwanted shareholders. But because shareholders want to balance protection on the one hand with liquidity on the other, the agreement will outline exceptions, allowing for some permitted transfers. Other provisions for share transfers include right of first offer, right of first refusal, tag-along rights and drag-along rights.

Permitted Transfer of Shares

Shareholder agreements typically allow for transfers that may become necessary for tax planning purposes. Correspondingly, shareholder agreements usually include provisions to permit the transfer of shares held by corporations to an affiliate or, where the shareholder is an individual, to family members or a fiduciary acting for the shareholder.

Right of First Offer

Under this provision (a ROFO), a shareholder wanting to sell shares must first offer them to the other existing shareholders. Only if the existing shareholders decline can the selling shareholder offer the shares to a third party. An offer made to a third party cannot be more favourable than the offer made to the existing shareholders.

Right of First Refusal

Under the right of first refusal (ROFR), a selling shareholder is obliged to obtain an acceptable bona fide offer from an arm's length party. With this offer in hand, the selling shareholder then approaches the existing shareholders, who have the option to purchase the shares on a pro rata basis on the terms outlined in the third-party offer. If all existing shareholders refuse the offer, then the selling shareholder can sell the shares to the third party, on the same terms.

> ▶ **DEFINITION**
>
> **Arm's Length Dealings:** Interactions between two parties that are independent of each other, without any special relationship.

A ROFR has the advantage that the shareholders get a feel for the market value of the shares. The selling shareholder, however, might not obtain a third party's best offer. Knowing there is a ROFR in place, the third party may be concerned about being used just to establish a price between the selling shareholder and the one holding the ROFR. As a result, the third party will likely offer a discounted price for the shares. Furthermore, the selling shareholder will have to spend time and money negotiating the potential transaction.

Tag-along ("Piggyback") Rights

Tag-along rights entitle shareholders, on a pro rata basis, to "tag along," or partici-pate in, any third-party share purchase offer made to the majority shareholders. This provision protects minority shareholders.

Drag-along Rights

Drag-along rights are the opposite of tag-along rights. They typically entitle a majority shareholder, upon receipt of a bona fide, arm's length share purchase offer they want to accept, to drag along the minority shareholders — in other words, to force them to sell their shares. The majority shareholder may be moti-vated to exercise these rights if selling all of the company shares results in a higher share purchase price. This provision serves majority shareholders.

Pre-emption Rights

Pre-emption rights ensure that shareholders cannot be diluted by the company issuing more shares. They allow the shareholders to participate, on a pro rata basis, in a new offering of shares, options or warrants from treasury. Frequently, pre-emption rights are granted with certain conditions, such as the following:

- Only shareholders above a certain ownership threshold (e.g., 5%) may be privy to pre-emption rights. Shareholders who drop below that threshold lose these rights.
- Pre-emption rights may not be triggered by shares issued under the company's stock option plan, or by conversion of preferred shares or convertible debentures existing as of the date of the shareholder agreement.
- Pre-emption rights may cease to apply to shareholders who are founders or employees when their employment comes to an end.

Exit Alternatives

A shareholder agreement will often provide multiple ways for shareholders to exit (or be required to exit) the corporation, including transfer of shares (as dis-cussed on page 32), as well as put and call options, a shotgun clause or the right to request dissolution proceedings.

Put and Call Options

Under a put option, a shareholder can demand that the other existing shareholders (on a pro rata basis) or the company (in the event of cancellation) purchase his or her shares at a specified price, allowing the shareholder to exit. The holder of a call option — which may be a single shareholder, a group of shareholders or the company — has the right to request the seller's shares at a predetermined price, forcing the shareholder to exit.

The owner of a put or call option may choose to exercise it after a certain period of time has elapsed, or the option may be triggered by a specific event, such as a shareholder's death or inability to participate in the company's affairs because of severe long-term disability or bankruptcy. In the case of an employee shareholder, retirement or other termination of employment may trigger the put or call option. A call option may also be an appropriate measure if a shareholder is in ongoing material breach of the shareholder agreement.

Shotgun Clause (Buy-Sell Provision)

A shotgun clause, also known as a buy-sell provision, is usually negotiated in a case where there are two 50/50 shareholders. It stipulates that the shareholder who is interested in a change of ownership will have to make two offers at the same time, on identical terms: an offer to buy all of the other shareholder's shares and an offer to sell all of his or her shares to the other shareholder. The shareholder receiving the offers must then decide which one to accept.

This approach is intended to ensure that the shareholder making the offers submits terms that are fair, to help resolve whatever disagreement initiated the process. The fairness of the transaction, however, can sometimes be jeopardized by an imbalance in the parties' negotiation power. For example, one shareholder may be better equipped to assess and finance the transaction or to run the business without the other shareholder. Solutions for these potential inequities should be considered when drafting this clause.

Right to Request Dissolution Proceedings

As an exit alternative of last resort, the shareholder agreement may include the right to seek the company's liquidation. This right is sometimes invoked in cases where there is an impasse among the shareholders.

Funding Arrangements

There are several provisions one should consider addressing when laying out funding arrangements in the shareholder agreement.

> ▶ **DEFINITION**
>
> **Capital Call:** A request from the company for equity injections from the shareholders.

Capital Call Provisions

Capital call provisions allow the board to ask shareholders to provide the company, on a pro rata basis, with additional funds in the form of equity injections, loans or other assets, such as property or equipment, or by way of guarantees. A guarantee would be given with the purpose of covering company obligations to third parties. As capital calls are generally made when the company is not performing as anticipated or the fundraising process is not evolving as planned, the risk increases for shareholders when this provision is included in the agreement.

Pre-emption Rights and Anti-dilution

As discussed on page 33, shareholders want to protect themselves from future dilutions through pre-emption rights, which allow them to participate, on a pro rata basis, in a new offering of shares, options or warrants from treasury. Investors who have purchased Preferred Series A Stock financings are typically successful in negotiating extensive anti-dilution protection mechanisms. But before we look at the details of such mechanisms, it is important to understand conversion rights.

Preferred shares may be convertible into common shares at the preferred shareholder's request, and certain qualifying events — such as the company's IPO or a merger with another corporation — may trigger an automatic conversion. An automatic conversion can also be initiated by vote of a specific percentage of shareholders. In addition, some shareholder agreements include a provision allowing the company to force a conversion of preferred shares into common shares, subject to certain conditions being met.

In cooperation with its advisors, and before issuing the preferred shares, management determines the ratio at which preferred shares will be converted into common shares. The conversion price is the price per share at which the preferred shares can be converted into common shares.

Some preferred shares are equipped with a "pay-to-play" provision: Preferred shareholders are required to buy their pro rata share in future share offerings to retain their preferences. Should they opt not to buy their pro rata share, their preferred shares will be converted into either common shares or another class of preferred shares that does not provide the desired anti-dilution protection. Pay-to-play provisions are used to motivate current investors to inject further capital in future funding rounds.

Preferred share provisions almost always include dilution protection from new share offerings through events such as stock splits or recapitalizations. In the case of venture capital financings, they tend to also protect against future issuances of shares at a price that is lower than the price paid by the preferred shareholder. This form of dilution protection is known as a "price-based anti-dilution provision in down rounds." There are two basic price-based anti-dilution provisions: a weighted average adjustment and a full ratchet adjustment.

Weighted Average Adjustment

Should the company issue shares at a purchase price below the conversion price of the previous preferred share round (here, Series A), the conversion price will be weighted by the shares that are being sold, allowing for an adjustment in accordance with the following formula:

$$CP_2 = CP_1 \times [(A + B) \div (A + C)]$$

Where:

CP_2 = Series A conversion price in effect just after a new issue

CP_1 = Series A conversion price in effect just before the new issue

A = Number of shares of common stock deemed to be outstanding right before the new issue, on a fully diluted basis (i.e., it includes all shares of outstanding common stock, all shares of outstanding preferred stock on an as-converted basis and all outstanding options on an as-exercised basis)

B = Aggregate consideration received by the corporation with respect to the new issue, divided by CP_1

C = Number of shares issued in the subject transaction

For example, if:

$$CP_1 = \$10$$
$$A = 1{,}000$$
$$B = (100 \times \$7.50) \div \$10 = 75$$
$$C = 100$$

Then:

$$CP_2 = \$10 \times [(1{,}000 + 75) \div (1{,}000 + 100)] = \$9.77$$

Full Ratchet Adjustment

In this less company-friendly alternative, the conversion price will be reduced to the price at which the new shares are being issued, no matter how many shares are being sold.

For example:

Using the same numbers as above, CP_2 = \$7.50

INSIDER TIP ▶ If possible, common shareholders should avoid the full ratchet adjustment, as it can be exceedingly dilutive to their shares. If avoidance is impossible, a time limit of, say, one year may be an acceptable alternative.

Venture Capital Traps

Here is how the shareholders of early-stage companies can get into trouble when agreeing to a Preferred Series A Stock financing and its extensive anti-dilution provisions. Often, young companies, requiring additional equity to grow to a stage where they are self-sufficient, will concede a substantial share of their company. They accept extensive anti-dilution protection mechanisms, along with drag-along rights, in the quest of making their dream come true, and they believe they will not need additional money, rendering the perils of a Preferred Series A Stock financing ineffective. However, they frequently do end up needing additional funds, because of delays or additional costs to execute the patent strategy, or for various other reasons. In the next fundraising round, the common shareholders (founders, friends and family, employees) may be diluted extensively, as they lack the anti-dilution protections that the Preferred Series A shareholders enjoy. This may even lead to the common shareholders being reduced to a minority, losing control. In that case, if the Preferred Series A shareholders come across an opportunity to sell the company at a price they find attractive, they can drag along the minority common shareholders even if they do not want to sell.

INSIDER TIP ▶ Watch out for anti-dilution provisions in Preferred Series A Stock financings, and carefully review any liquidation preferences. Stay away from full participating preferred stock, and avoid scenarios whereby the preferred shareholders are entitled to a multiple of their whole investment before any remaining proceeds are distributed to common shareholders.

Another point to focus on is the liquidation preference, usually encountered in Preferred Series A Stock financings. It determines how the company shall distribute proceeds from certain specified events, commonly liquidation, dissolution, merger or change of control.

There are three liquidation preferences: non-participating preferred stock, full participating preferred stock and capped or partially participating preferred stock.

Non-participating Preferred Stock
In this scenario, preferred shareholders are entitled to the return of their whole investment, plus accrued dividends, before any remaining proceeds are being distributed to the common shareholders. This liquidation preference is most favourable to the common shareholders.

Full Participating Preferred Stock
Once the preferred shareholders have received their whole investment, plus accrued dividends, they share equally, on a pro rata basis, with the common shareholders in the remaining proceeds, as if the preferred shareholders had converted their shares to common shares. In other words, the preferred shareholders participate twice, which is why this alternative is sometimes called "double-dip preferred stock." This liquidation preference is most favourable to the preferred shareholders.

Capped or Partially Participating Preferred Stock
Once the preferred shareholders have received their whole investment, plus accrued dividends, they share equally, on a pro rata basis, with the common shareholders in the remaining proceeds, but only up to a certain amount. Over and above that amount, the common shareholders do not have to share any proceeds with the preferred shareholders.

Preferred share investors will also sometimes negotiate a "multiple," whereby they are entitled to a multiple (2x, 3x, and so on) of their investment plus accrued dividends before any remaining proceeds are distributed to the common shareholders.

As an illustration of the consequences of the type of liquidation preference you should avoid, let's assume you have sold your company for $15 million. There are no creditors, and no unpaid dividends. The Preferred Series A Stock financing was for $5 million for 50% of the company. As you were left with little other choice, you agreed to full participating preferred shares with a 2x multiple. Correspondingly, the preferred shareholders now receive $10 million (two times their investment) plus, in accordance with their 50% ownership, another $2.5 million of the remaining $5 million, for a total of $12.5 million, or 83% of total proceeds, for their 50% ownership. By contrast, the common shareholders collect just $2.5 million, or 17% of total proceeds, for their 50% ownership.

Non-competition and Non-solicitation Agreements

Some investors may require founders and key employees to enter into non-competition and non-solicitation agreements. A non-compete clause usually stipulates that the one party will not enter into any business that would compete with the other party. A non-solicitation clause restricts the one party from soliciting employees, customers and business opportunities from the other party. These agreements typically have a one-year duration, but in some cases last up to two years, or possibly even longer.

Accredited Investors

In general, securities must be sold by prospectus unless there is an available exemption. One of these exemptions is the sale of shares to an accredited investor (also called a qualified investor).

Accredited investors are certain institutions, persons and companies, as defined in the regulation of the relevant jurisdiction, that are deemed sophisticated and, as such, not in need of the protection a prospectus offers. These investors can 1) source and analyze the information required to assess an investment without a prospectus, and 2) handle the loss of their entire investment if things go wrong. Accredited investors typically include governments or governmental agencies, financial institutions, insurance companies, pension funds, registered charities, registered market dealers, companies whose net assets exceed certain thresholds, and individuals whose net worth or annual income exceeds certain thresholds.

If an issuer of the securities is relying on an exemption, the onus is on the issuer to ensure compliance with the securities legislation. If a registered market dealer is involved, then the onus is on both the issuer and the dealer. The stock purchase agreement (also called a subscription agreement) typically stipulates that the purchaser of the stock must be an accredited investor, as defined in the relevant securities act of the jurisdiction in question.

The regulation must be carefully considered when raising equity via private placement. There can be severe consequences for not complying properly. Legal counsel should be involved.

Valuation

The question of the value of shares — and by extension the value of the company — arises every time shares are issued or transferred, whether as part of the company's fundraising efforts, in the case of a capital call, or as the result of an exit.

In the market, there are essentially four approaches to assessing a company's value: EBITDA multiple, net present value, a combination of EBITDA multiple and net present value, or value creation. Shareholders may agree to one of these approaches in the shareholder agreement, or they may settle on another way to arrive at the share value, as discussed on page 43.

> ▶ **DEFINITION**
>
> **EBITDA:** EBITDA (earnings before interest, taxes, depreciation and amortization) means net income before extraordinary or other non-recurring items for a certain period, *plus*, to the extent deducted in determining net income for that period, the sum of interest expense, tax expense and depreciation, amortization and other non-cash charges; *minus* any non-cash credits for that period.

In Practice

In practice, there are two main approaches to assessing a company's value: applying an EBITDA multiple or calculating the net present value. These two methods can also be combined. Furthermore, the value of a company can be derived from the milestones that have been met since the most recent valuation.

EBITDA Multiple

Experienced investors who are familiar with the company's sector will likely use an EBITDA multiple, or sometimes a revenue multiple, that is in line with the multiple of comparable publicly traded companies or of recent comparable transactions. For example, let's say various publicly traded companies in the same sector have a market capitalization of four to six times their normalized EBITDA; in other words, their EBITDA multiple is 4–6x. EBITDA is normalized when it is net of extraordinary items. Furthermore, a comparable company was recently acquired at 5 times its normalized EBITDA. So, in this example, the company's value may be assessed as 4–6x normalized EBITDA.

> ▶ **DEFINITION**
>
> **Market Capitalization:** Number of shares of a publicly traded company multiplied by the price per share, amounting to the total value of the shares.

Should the company be at an early stage without any or many comparables in the same industry, the experienced investor will suggest a multiple that is in line with the multiples the investor paid to acquire other companies in the investor's portfolio.

Investors will often focus on the company's EBITDA at two points in time: 1) before the equity raise (also called pre-money), and 2) in year 2 or 3, subject to the investor believing in the company's projected growth. The investor will want those two numbers to be similar. For example, the investor may buy into a pre-money valuation of 4–6x EBITDA corresponding to a 2–3x EBITDA in year 2.

So if pre-money EBITDA is $5 million, the company's value amounts to $20–30 million (4–6× $5 million). For year 2, EBITDA is projected to be $10 million, resulting in a valuation of $20–30 million (2–3× $10 million), a range that is in line with the pre-money valuation.

Net Present Value

Another approach frequently applied in practice is to calculate the net present value (NPV) of the company's projected cash flow stream. It makes particular sense when assessing the value of a company or project with a certain project life. This method requires that the negotiating parties largely agree on the projections and the discount factor used to arrive at the net present value.

Combination of EBITDA Multiple and Net Present Value

In determining the valuation of a company whose business life does not end after a specific period of time, a combination of EBITDA and NPV is often used. One would calculate the NPV of the company's cash flow stream for, say, the first three years and add to it the company's value in year 3, which, in turn, is determined by an EBITDA multiple suitable for the industry and acceptable to the negotiating parties.

Value Creation

Another valuation method considers the share prices that were established in previous equity financing rounds and the value the company has created since.

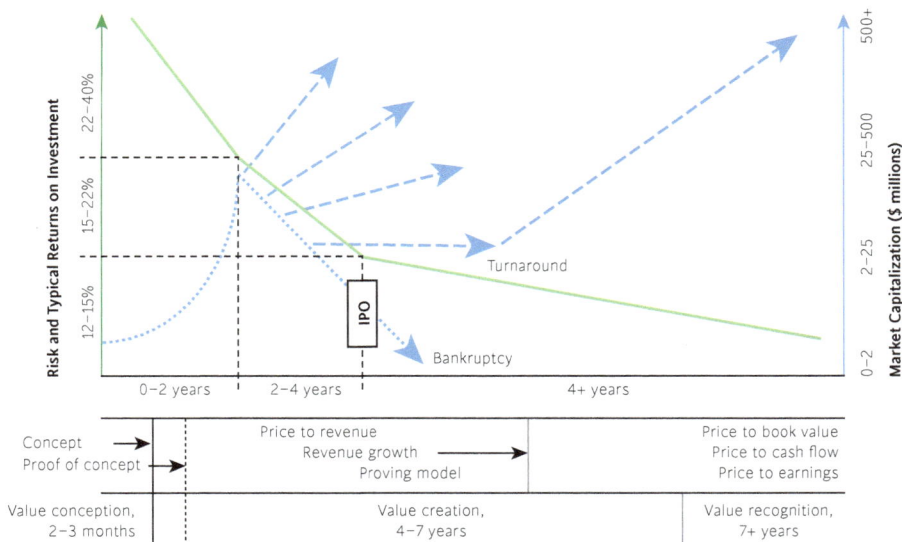

FIGURE 7: TRADITIONAL VALUE CREATION PROFILE

Source: WRTharp — The Climate Change Infrastructure Corporation. Used with permission.

Assuming the company has met crucial milestones since the most recent equity round, it can make a strong argument that the share price of this financing round should be higher than it was in the past round. If, for example, the company recently raised funds at $0.30 per share and has since secured further patents, streamlined its manufacturing process and won some purchase orders, it has a strong case for asking for a higher share price.

Figure 7 (page 41) illustrates a traditional value creation profile for a company's progression from conception to a mature, value-oriented company.

In the earlier years of a company, investors will give the business greater latitude and not apply "hard" valuation requirements. Correspondingly, investors will see value in and pay for high revenue growth, larger margins or a theme wherein the new business is changing the entire pricing dynamics in an industry.

Challenges arise when revenue growth lessens, margins tighten or the industry starts to adapt to the new business and price competitively. This is when the company's growth profile (reflected in the above figure as market capitalization) eases. The company is now at a critical point. Will it make the transition to a mature company where different valuation metrics are applied (price to book value, price to cash flow or return on invested equity), or will it fail? If the company cannot maintain its value under the pricing metrics for more mature companies, it will not be able to raise the equity required for its growth and success, and it will go bankrupt.

Equity raised through an initial public offering or through other means will help the company over the gap from early stage to maturity.

Valuation Guidelines

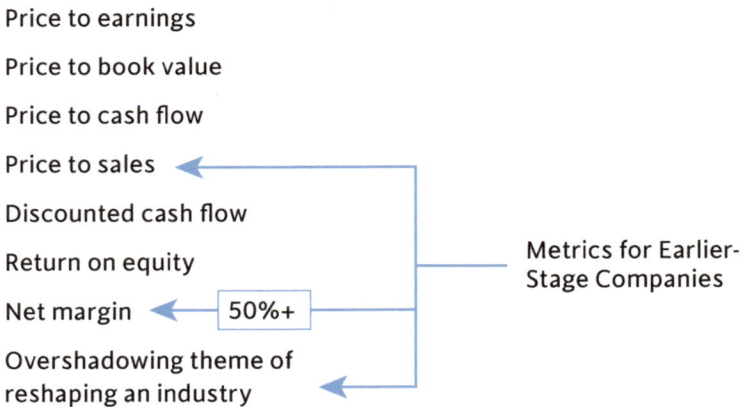

Price to earnings

Price to book value

Price to cash flow

Price to sales

Discounted cash flow

Return on equity

Net margin — 50%+

Overshadowing theme of reshaping an industry

Metrics for Earlier-Stage Companies

FIGURE 8: EARLY-STAGE VALUATION GUIDELINES

Source: WRTharp — The Climate Change Infrastructure Corporation. Used with permission.

Valuation Guidelines

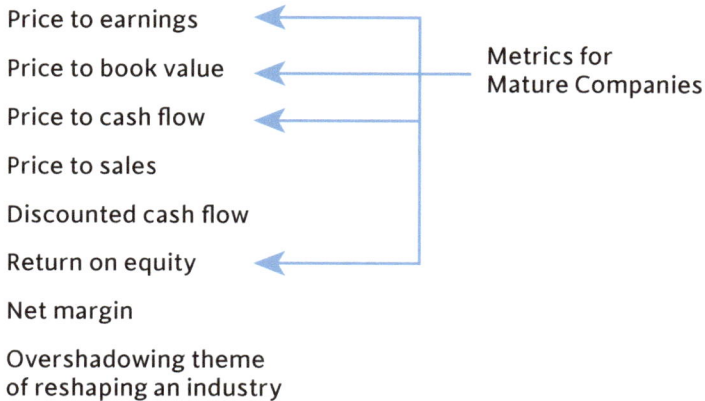

Price to earnings

Price to book value

Price to cash flow

Price to sales

Discounted cash flow

Return on equity

Net margin

Overshadowing theme
of reshaping an industry

Metrics for
Mature Companies

FIGURE 9: MATURE VALUATION GUIDELINES

Source: WRTharp — *The Climate Change Infrastructure Corporation. Used with permission.*

Figures 8 and 9 illustrate the valuation guidelines for earlier-stage and mature companies.

In the Shareholder Agreement

There are three principal methods that can be used in a shareholder agreement to determine the exit price or the price of new shares being issued as part of an equity raise: calculations based on a formula, agreement among the shareholders or determination by a third party.

Calculations Based on a Formula

In this approach, the company valuation is based on one of the formulas discussed on pages 40–41. It is important to involve your accountant when settling on a formula.

Agreement among the Shareholders

The shareholders simply consent to have the company valuated on a regular basis, perhaps annually or biannually. This method tends to be a less effective option, however, as a company valuation is an involved process and shareholders often let it slide when they feel they have more pressing things on their agenda.

Determination by a Third Party

The shareholders agree to retain a third party to provide a business valuation. That third party would typically be a chartered business valuator, investment banker or accountant.

Equity Financing

Early-Stage Heavy Water Manufacturer Raising Equity for Disruptive Technology

Challenge: Capital needed to get ready for a bigger financing round (i.e., this raise was one financing round removed from generating revenues)

Solutions:
- Seek strategic partners for product offtake and lead investment
- Attract high-net-worth individuals as investors
- Secure interim revenues to attract investors

Private placement: $1–3 million

Proceeds used for: Expansion of intellectual property, alignment of supply chain, hiring of additional staff, working capital

The challenge of this fundraising mandate lay in this early-stage company requiring interim funds before the next, larger financing round, which would get it to cash flow break-even. In other words, the investor was going to be one financing round removed from revenue generation. This is not an attractive proposition for investors, outside of venture capital investors, and venture capital investors were excluded to prevent any Preferred Series A Stock financings.

Working closely with our client, who has strong relationships with various players in his market, we were able to attract a strategic partner as a lead investor and potential purchaser of our client's products. Furthermore, our client was able to create an interim business with revenues by trading the type of products the company will be manufacturing and distributing in a few years.

Having secured a lead investor who understood the market, the technology and the business opportunity, and having grasped a short-term revenue-generating opportunity, our client was now an attractive investment for high-net-worth individuals. Because of the anticipated difficulties with raising equity for this client, we had approached the market with a private placement range of $1–3 million, and eventually closed the transaction at $800,000. This raise has put our client in the position of reaching cash flow break-even and it allowed him to meet certain milestones (such as the completion and successful operation of a demonstration project, expansion of intellectual property registration and alignment of the supply chain), which, in turn, enables the company to approach the market for the larger fundraising.

CHAPTER THREE

DEBT FINANCING

What Is Debt Financing?

Debt financing refers to funds a lender provides based on predetermined terms and conditions, such as purpose of the loan, term, principal repayment, interest payment, collateral, representations and covenants. In other words, the parties know exactly how much the loan is for, when the loan is to be repaid and what the return (or interest) on the loan is.

Recourse versus Non-recourse Financing

One primary differentiator between the types of debt financing is the question of recourse to the borrower. If the lender has recourse, it has the right to collect from all of the borrower's assets — not just from the ones the loan financed. In other words, the borrower's entire balance sheet is available to the lender to recover outstanding principal and interest payments. Correspondingly, the loan will be reflected on the borrower's balance sheet. This type of financing is also called on-balance sheet financing.

A non-recourse loan prevents the lender from collecting from anybody or anything outside of the asset the loan is based on. The asset owner's (or sponsor's) whole balance sheet is not available for recovery of the loan. The loan is collateralized (secured) against specific assets and the cash flows that the assets produce. It is based on the quality of the asset and its future cash flows, and not on the creditworthiness or balance sheet of the sponsor. Correspondingly, the non-recourse loan is not reflected on the sponsor's balance sheet; but the sponsor's investment in the asset is documented on the balance sheet. This type of financing is also called off-balance sheet financing. Project financing is a form of non-recourse lending. It is discussed beginning on page 51.

Types of Lenders

This book focuses on institutional lenders, which are, for our purposes, regulated entities that loan money, specifically banks, pension funds and life insurance companies. In addition, leasing companies regularly finance equipment and projects through financial leases. As this is a practical alternative to long-term loans, it is discussed on page 77.

Banks

Banks are frequently accused of not being supportive enough, of handing out umbrellas when the sun is shining and collecting them when it is raining. To better understand how bankers think and why they act the way they do, let's consider the role of banks in the financial system and the economy.

At the most basic level, a bank functions by borrowing money from some people and lending it to others, thereby taking on important transformation services that lead to an efficient and prosperous economy and improved standards of living:

Transformation of Amounts
Banks harmonize the diverging requirements of savers and borrowers by accumulating many small deposits and then loaning funds in larger amounts. They also do the opposite by accepting large deposits and making smaller loans.

Transformation of Maturity
Banks assign one set of terms and interest periods for the deposits they accept, and a very different set of terms for the loans they advance.

Transformation of Risk
When loaning funds, banks dramatically reduce their depositors' risk of loss by using sophisticated and proven standards to assess a borrower's creditworthiness, and by ensuring that their portfolios are diversified.

Transformation of Information
By providing the necessary information, banks spare savers and borrowers the time, effort and cost of searching for a suitable counterparty on their own.

Transformation of Geographic Markets
Banks gather funds from and distribute funds to different regions of a country and throughout the world, creating hubs where supply and demand can meet.

Furthermore, banks provide vital payment and settlement services; they are the backup source of liquidity for all financial institutions; and they create money when advancing loans, as they are permitted to loan multiple times the amount of their equity. In addition, reserve banks control the supply of money within the economy, using targets and indicators that are, to a large extent, associated with banking institutions.

> ▶ **DEFINITION**
>
> **Sweet Spot:** A loan that hits a bank's sweet spot will meet all the criteria the bank prefers, such as a solid return, low to moderate risk and straightforward terms and conditions. It will also involve an industry that is well understood, even targeted, by the bank, and a loan amount that fits in the bank's preferred range.

The Bank's Psyche
Let us get deeper into the psyche of a bank by discussing what motivates a lender. First off, a lender will go after low-hanging fruit — familiar industries, a proven

track record of financial performance (which usually means three years), collateral of easily measurable value — so it can assess risks and return with little effort. A banker will pursue transactions that are in the bank's sweet spot and promise solid yields. As these opportunities are exhausted, the bank will be prepared to slowly move away from the sweet spot and consider more complex and riskier transactions at the appropriate risk-adjusted return on capital. In times of great competition, banks have proven to be creative with offerings at the fringe or even outside of their core to attract business. Should the bank experience a shock to its system through exceptional events, such as the burst of the dot-com bubble or the subprime mortgage crises, it will instantly withdraw to its core business and core risk appetite. Imagine a pendulum inching its way slowly to one side, only to swing back very quickly during a crisis. The process then repeats itself, very slowly. This sequence of events is largely driven by the bank's credit assessment. The credit committee tends to gradually become more comfortable with certain risks. The more impact an event has on the bank, the more quickly its credit committee returns to the basics.

Considering how bankers think, it is advisable to secure a loan, perhaps in a larger amount than required, in good times, as it will be very difficult to attract one in a more difficult environment.

> **INSIDER TIP ▶** Put a loan or line of credit in place when your business is doing well, perhaps in a larger amount than required.

It is also important to understand what is at the heart of a bank's evaluation of a borrower's creditworthiness. Central to that investigation are the three Cs: competence, cash flow and collateral — in that order. First and foremost, the bank wants to be comfortable with the borrower's expertise in running the business and with the quality of the products/services and technology. The bank's assessment revolves around the borrower's ability to repay the loan; hence, the bank will make great effort to properly understand the borrower's cash flow, past, present and future. Only if the bank is satisfied with competence and cash flow will it consider the collateral. In reality, this happens simultaneously, but the message is that a bank will not agree to a loan transaction that provides fabulous collateral but lacks the bank's approval with respect to competence and cash flow.

Banks (and other lenders) do not easily immerse themselves in new industries. They will stay within their comfort zone as long as possible, going outside it only if competitive forces push them out or attractive returns elsewhere pull them out. There will have to be enough money in the new sector for the bank to go through the effort to learn about it and assess the risks. This can be a slow process, and borrowers may become impatient with it. But borrowers need to appreciate that they are trying to attract money from lenders that have a choice, and that the banks do not know the market, business and players as well as the borrowers. When they do venture into a new market, banks will approach the transactions conservatively, with tighter terms and conditions than usual, until they are more familiar with the risks.

The Golden Bank Rule

The Golden Bank Rule (or Golden Financing Rule) states that long-term assets should be financed long-term (with equity and long-term debt).

To understand the importance of this rule, let's look at a simplified example. Say a manufacturer wants to buy a new machine to cater to the demand it is experiencing. The desired equipment, including transport and installation, costs $1 million. The manufacturer has $500,000 cash in the bank and plenty of room under its line of credit of $1.5 million. The line of credit is margined against the manufacturer's accounts receivable, but, thanks to the company's cash position, it has hardly been used. The manufacturer believes the new machine will increase revenues, thereby improving its cash position even further, and that it will require no more than $1 million for working capital. This sum includes the financing of the additional purchase orders and the raw materials needed to operate the new machine.

First question: Should the manufacturer use its cash and line of credit to finance the capital expenditure, considering that its liquidity is favourable and more cash is expected to come in soon? Or should it secure a five-year term loan, in line with the machine's expected useful life?

According to the Golden Bank Rule, the manufacturer should go for the term loan. But let's consider a potential scenario should the manufacturer decide to use its cash of $500,000 and draw another $500,000 from its line of credit, giving it $1 million of working capital. As the machine is being installed, the manufacturer experiences significant delays with the machine's integration into the production process, though the machine itself works fine. During this time, the demand for the manufacturer's products unexpectedly softens, which, in turn, reduces the company's accounts receivable. The available funds in the line of credit quickly melt away for the following reasons:

- Because the line of credit is margined against the company's accounts receivable, the maximum drawdown limit is now reduced thanks to the decline in accounts receivable.
- The manufacturer used funds from the line of credit to acquire raw materials to feed the new machine; this raw material now sits in inventory while the production delays are sorted out.
- Fixed operating expenses (such as wages and rent) are ongoing.

This scenario illustrates why cash reserves and lines of credit should be used to finance raw materials and purchase orders, and to bridge revenue fluctuations, but not to finance long-term assets. Not only has the manufacturer's liquidity tightened up, but it is in a much weaker position to secure a term loan and will likely receive less favourable terms. Putting the proper financing in place will now cost the company extra money, time and energy.

INSIDER TIP ▶ The terms and conditions of a loan secured in good times will be more favourable than those of a loan negotiated in challenging times.

Second question: If the company has cash in the bank, why take out a loan and pay interest?

Only if the company will not require the cash in the bank in the long term does it make sense to use it to finance the machine. Otherwise, the cash should be used as a liquidity reserve. Liquidity has to trump return.

In this context, also consider the company's weighted average cost of capital (WACC), the weighted average rate it pays to the company's funders on all equity and debt instruments. By taking out a loan instead of using cash, the company may be able to reduce its WACC and increase its return.

INSIDER TIP ▶ Follow the Golden Bank Rule every time you are financing a capital expenditure.

Bank Regulation

Banks are subject to different regulation than pension funds and life insurance companies, in that they are required to allocate a certain amount of their capital to each loan they commit to. The longer the term of the loan or the higher the risk of the transaction (determined through an internal risk rating process), the more capital the bank will have to allocate. This is one of the reasons why banks prefer to cap their long-term lending at five to eight years. Due to this regulation, the banks' capital tends to be more expensive than that of life insurance companies or pension funds.

Other Lenders

Pension funds and life insurance companies are also important lenders. They often do not deal directly with the borrower but participate in syndications (see page 76) or lend through the engagement of intermediaries. When dealing with the borrower directly, they tend to provide larger financings, usually in the areas of infrastructure or public-private partnerships.

Project Financing

Project financing has evolved as a leading way to finance renewable energy and clean technology projects. Historically, project financing was developed to finance large infrastructure projects off-balance sheet that might otherwise have been too large or risky to be carried on a corporate balance sheet. Today, these types of undertakings are still financed through project financing. They tend to be in the $50–$100 million range, at a minimum, and they are being executed by sophisticated people on both the lenders' and sponsor's sides of the transaction.

This book does not address these traditional project financings. Instead, in the interest of the less experienced borrower, it examines smaller versions of project financing that have emerged, especially in the areas of renewable energy (energy generation from renewable sources, such as wind, sunlight, biomass, biogas and municipal waste) and clean technology (technology that reduces the carbon footprint).

What Is Project Financing?

With project financing, lenders base their loans for the construction of a project on the specific risks of the project, its assets and its future cash flows. A key goal is to have this financing be off-balance sheet — that is, without recourse to the parent company that develops (or sponsors) the project. In that case, significant liabilities stay off the sponsor's balance sheet, thereby protecting key assets. Correspondingly, a project loan is secured against all project assets, including the revenue-producing contracts and the pledge of all equity interest in the project/borrower.

That said, some limited recourse is often created through a sponsor support and completion guarantee agreement (or sponsor support agreement) for the construction period of the project. Under such an agreement, the sponsor agrees to make additional specified equity contributions as required to pay project costs (such as construction cost overruns or fixed costs including debt service during construction) should there be a shortfall in the construction budget, so as not to jeopardize final completion of the project at the guaranteed performance levels and timelines. The sponsor will typically negotiate a cap on such obligations. Commonly, the lender will require that the sponsor support agreement is backed by a letter of credit in a form and substance satisfactory to the lender and issued by a bank satisfactory to the lender.

Project financing is also a way to finance still new but proven technologies. The manufacturer of the technology may be relatively young, with weak financials marked by this stage of development. Such a manufacturer might be faced with two challenges:

1. It cannot raise debt, as it lacks proven financial performance and probably the balance sheet strength necessary for a favourable assessment of its creditworthiness. Due to the project's larger size, it may not be feasible to finance the whole project through equity.
2. Despite having a number of smaller equity-financed versions of its technology operating successfully in a commercial setting (where they are economical), the manufacturer may require revenues from the sale of larger, scaled-up versions of that technology to strengthen its financial position. The company may have difficulty attracting clients that are prepared to take this scale-up risk, and it may find it challenging to secure the working capital needed to fund the production of the technology.

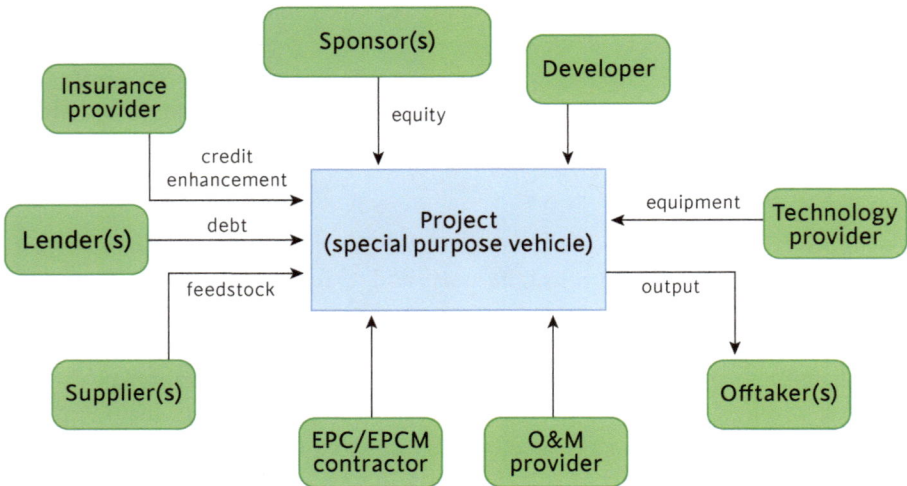

FIGURE 10: SIMPLIFIED PROJECT FINANCING STRUCTURE

Project financing may be the solution to the manufacturer's predicament. As seen in the wind and then solar industries, manufacturers had to become developers of projects for a period of time, using their own technology to demonstrate its quality and, consequently, to create demand and grow the business.

If the project meets the key requirements for project financing, such as experienced management, proven technology and long-term supply and offtake (or output purchase) agreements with creditworthy parties (as discussed further in Key Requirements, below), money can be raised. A project is self-contained and, hence, easier for a lender to assess.

Figure 10 shows a simplified overview of a project financing structure, with its main service providers and stakeholders. Some of the roles may be filled by the same entity. For example, the sponsor may also be the developer and/or the engineering, procurement and construction (EPC) contractor and/or the operations and maintenance (O&M) provider.

Key Requirements

Figure 11 outlines the main criteria that a lender prefers to see fulfilled for the advancement of project financing. Project management is "proven" when it is experienced in this type of activity, with a solid track record of success to show for it. Technology is proven when it has already been deployed in commercial settings and has had documented economic and operational success, without any issues or, if there were issues, with evidence that they have been overcome.

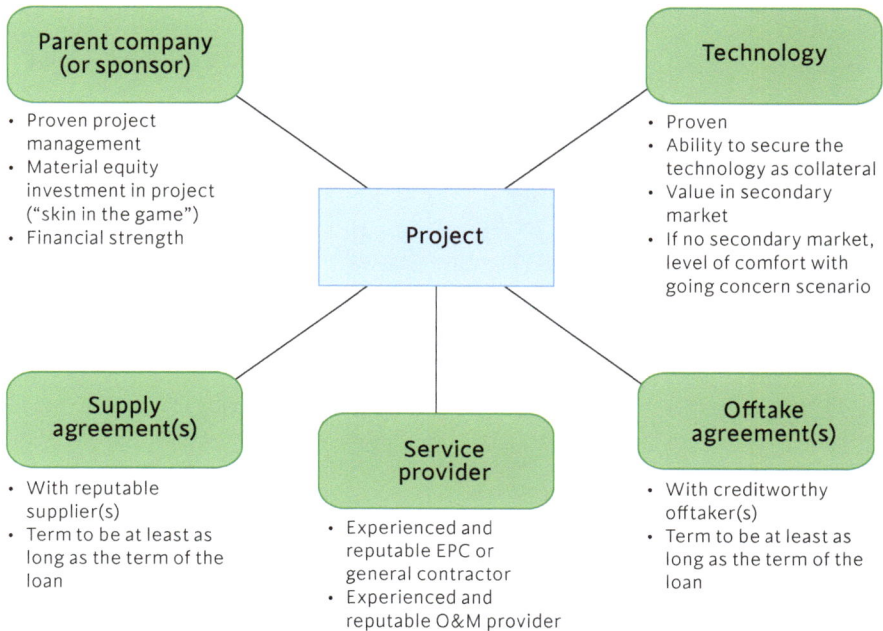

FIGURE 11: A PROJECT FINANCIER'S PREFERRED CRITERIA

As discussed on page 52, the parent company may not yet exhibit financial strength. Or perhaps long-term supply agreements are not yet available in the industry. Perhaps the technology in question has been proven in smaller applications but not on the scale now being contemplated. In the last scenario, where the technology is being scaled up without a precedent, an independent engineer (chosen by the lender) may give the lender the comfort required. The lender may also compensate for their reduced comfort with a lower leverage (or debt-to-total-capital ratio) and, perhaps, a higher maintenance reserve account. But how can a project become more attractive to a lender when the project's sponsor exhibits weak financials because the company is still young and growing? A project sponsor that is also a project developer can enhance its creditworthiness by:

- Choosing proven technology that comes with strong warranties from a creditworthy manufacturer;
- Making sure that replacement parts for the technology are readily available off the shelf;
- Securing vendor financing from a creditworthy manufacturer (subordinated to the lenders' debt) or having the manufacturer make an equity investment;
- Engaging an experienced and reputable EPC contractor with a solid balance sheet that grants satisfactory warranties;
- Hiring an experienced and reputable O&M provider;
- Concluding a long-term offtake agreement with a creditworthy purchaser of all of the project's production. The purchaser will likely also understand the technology risk. This will make the lender feel more comfortable;
- Accepting reduced leverage and, perhaps, higher reserve accounts.

▶ DEFINITION

Leverage: The amount of debt (to be) used to finance a company's assets, expressed as a percent of total capital (consisting of debt and equity).

Creditworthiness

A borrower is creditworthy when the lender comes to the conclusion that the borrower is able to service the debt (i.e., pay interest and principal as per the loan agreement). The conclusion is derived from an expansive due diligence investigation, which is discussed in detail on page 93.

Bankability of the Technology

In projects where technology plays a big role, such as in wind, solar, hydro and bio-energy projects, the technology's bankability (or financeability) is the starting point of the lenders' credit assessment.

But what does that mean? When is technology bankable? Figure 12 helps to provide the answers.

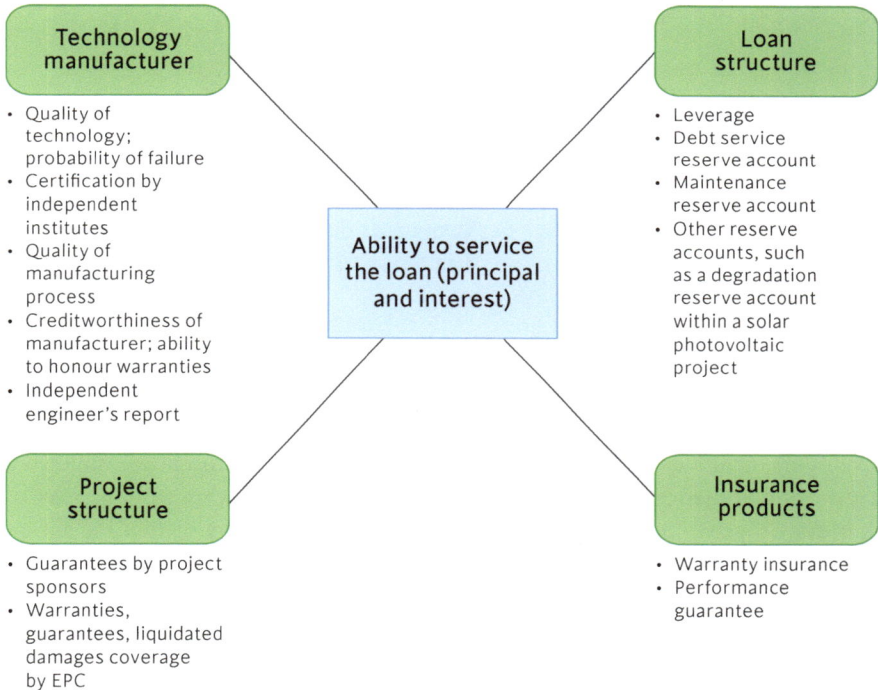

Technology manufacturer
- Quality of technology; probability of failure
- Certification by independent institutes
- Quality of manufacturing process
- Creditworthiness of manufacturer; ability to honour warranties
- Independent engineer's report

Loan structure
- Leverage
- Debt service reserve account
- Maintenance reserve account
- Other reserve accounts, such as a degradation reserve account within a solar photovoltaic project

Ability to service the loan (principal and interest)

Project structure
- Guarantees by project sponsors
- Warranties, guarantees, liquidated damages coverage by EPC

Insurance products
- Warranty insurance
- Performance guarantee

FIGURE 12: CRITERIA INFLUENCING BANKABILITY OF TECHNOLOGY

To attract project financing, a project has to procure technology that is bankable. Unfortunately, there is no standard set of deliverables a technology provider has to fulfill to be considered bankable. Each lender will have its own criteria, which are likely to change over time. That said, the technical requirements each lender looks for are more or less the same: quality of the technology and of the production process, certification of the technology, financial strength and projections of the manufacturer to honour warranties. An independent engineer will assess the technology and the manufacturing process, and prepare a report for the lender.

Again, a credit decision is made on many criteria, which are interactive. It is like a puzzle with alternate pieces that can come together to form a picture in different ways. Following are some of the pieces a lender may play with in order to come to a positive decision:

- Guarantees: Should there be some material weaknesses in the assessment of the technology, they may be mitigated through the project structure if it includes useful guarantees from the project sponsors and/or the EPC contractor;
- Leverage: A project that is not financeable at 75% debt, due to certain offtake or technology risks, may be financeable with 40–60% debt because the lenders are taking less risk with a higher level of capital prepaid into the project;
- Debt service, maintenance or other reserve accounts;
- Reports and opinions from experts, such as independent engineers, market consultants, environmental consultants and insurance consultants;
- Insurance products: For example, warranty insurance covering the manufacturer's warranties, or a performance guarantee that indemnifies (part of) the revenue stream of an installation for the term of the financing arrangement.

Large project sponsors might have the resources to finance the construction of a project from equity. Upon project completion, they would then refinance the project through project debt to free up most of their invested capital. Most developers, however, will endeavour to secure construction financing, followed, at project completion, by take-out (or term) financing. In this case, as part of their due diligence investigation, the lender will carefully review the EPC agreement and the EPC contractor's creditworthiness, especially with respect to its warranties. Lenders do not take on construction risk. Corporate parent guarantees, performance bonds or other forms of performance guarantees will have to be provided to assure lenders that project completion will happen within the guaranteed performance levels and timelines. A performance bond is typically issued by an insurance company or bank, and guarantees satisfactory completion of a project by the EPC contractor. It gives the recipient of the bond (the project owner and, by extension, the lender) comfort that a financial loss suffered from a contractor's event of default will be covered. Furthermore, the EPC contractor's warranties will have to satisfy the lenders that the project will not incur substantial unexpected expenses.

With respect to the structure of the agreement, lenders prefer a "full wrap" EPC contract, where the EPC contractor is the single point of contact for the lenders to interact with and take recourse to when it comes to covering the various risks the agreement addresses, such as performance and payment schedules, warranties and insurance, and performance guarantees. Lenders would rather not have to deal with an assortment of subcontractors, especially when new technology is involved. Lenders also look for satisfactory liquidated damage coverage in the EPC contract, meaning that the EPC contractor agrees to make payments upon specific breaches of the agreement, such as delays in performance or in meeting certain milestones, or equipment flaws. In summary, the amount of risk the EPC contractor is willing to accept has an impact on the financeability of the project.

Finally, a customized loan structure and insurance products may provide lenders with the comfort they require to conclude that the project's cash flow will be sufficient to service the debt. Warranty insurance and performance guarantees may be attractive insurance products with respect to project financing. However, it is important to fully understand the costs and exclusions of such policies. Clauses are sometimes included that prevent or limit the ability to make a claim, possibly rendering the policy useless from a lender's perspective.

> **INSIDER TIP ▶** It is crucial to understand the project lenders' requirements when negotiating offtake and EPC agreements. Investing in expert advice during the negotiation phase will pay off at the financing stage, saving you from having to renegotiate your offtake and EPC agreements and, hence, from spending additional time and money that could be used in the development of your project.

Loan Types

Project companies typically require four different types of loans: a construction loan, a term loan, a working capital loan and a letter of credit.

Construction Loans

As the name suggests, construction loans finance the construction of a project. They allow multiple drawdowns as specified milestones are met, subject to the lender's independent engineer certifying the achievement of these milestones. Construction loans and term loans often have the same interest rate, as a construction loan carries higher risk but has a shorter term, while a term loan carries lower risk but has a much longer term; in some cases, however, the interest rate for a construction loan will be higher, reflecting the higher risk. At the construction loan's maturity, it either converts into a term loan or is replaced by a term loan. The conversion is usually subject to "substantial" or "final" completion, as defined in the EPC agreement. Should the project not meet that milestone within a given timeframe, the borrower will be in default under the construction loan.

Term Loans

Term loans are typically disbursed in one drawdown, to refinance the construction loan or, where the construction has been financed through equity, the sponsor's equity. Term loans have clearly defined maturity dates, as well as repayment dates and amounts. Interest rates can be fixed or floating. The amortization period can go beyond the tenor of the loan.

> ### ▶ DEFINITION
>
> **Tenor:** The term of a loan, from effective date to maturity.

Working Capital Loans

In this context, working capital loans are significantly smaller than construction and term loans. They provide a means to finance ordinary expenses, such as inventory of raw materials or wages. They are generally margined against the project company's inventory and cash. Working capital loans are typically revolving, which means that they do not have a fixed drawdown or repayment schedule but can be drawn on as required, up to a specified amount, and that repaid amounts are available for drawdown again.

> ### ▶ DEFINITION
>
> **Drawdown Period:** The period during which a borrower is permitted to draw on a loan. After this period, no further drawdowns are allowed.

Letters of Credit

Letters of credit are issued by a financial institution as credit support on behalf of the project company. They guarantee a payment or service the project company has committed to provide to various third parties, such as to the EPC contractor under the EPC agreement (for payment) or to the purchaser of the project company's output under the offtake agreement (for services).

> ### ▶ DEFINITION
>
> **Offtake Agreement:** An agreement between the producer of a product and the buyer (or offtaker), outlining the terms and conditions of the relationship.

Selected Key Terms and Conditions

Project financing term sheets are quite comprehensive. The main terms and conditions are explained here.

Type of Financing and Use of Proceeds

The term sheet outlines that it is a senior secured first-priority non-recourse financing, consisting of construction and/or term loans and, perhaps, a working capital credit facility and a letter of credit facility. It also documents what the proceeds will (and cannot) be used for.

Borrower and Sponsor

The term sheet further defines who the borrower and sponsor are, and what sponsor support is required.

Tenor

The construction loan will cover the anticipated construction period. The term of the offtake agreement has an impact on the tenor of the term loan, as does the type of lender. Typically, the term loan will not have a tenor that exceeds the term of the offtake agreement. While banks tend to provide shorter terms, with five to seven years being considered long-term in North America, life insurance companies and pension funds prefer longer terms — often as long as the term of the underlying offtake agreement. Power purchase agreements, for example, often have a term of 20 years, while the offtake agreements with hydro plants may even have a term of up to 40 years. Correspondingly, life insurance companies and pension funds would provide loans with a term, fixed interest rate and amortization of up to 20 or 40 years, respectively.

> ▶ **DEFINITION**
>
> **Power Purchase Agreement:** An offtake agreement where the "product" is electricity.

Priority of Funding

Loans are usually available only after all equity and proceeds from subordinated financing (if any) have been applied to the project costs, though possibly only a notional second before the loans are to be applied.

It is worthwhile to note that a lender will only seriously entertain a financing if the equity is already secured or, at least, in advanced negotiations. The same applies to completion risk. There has to be a clear roadmap on how completion risk will be covered, as lenders will not take that risk themselves. Lenders will not provide a term sheet before these criteria are fulfilled, lest they be wasting their time. Also, a term sheet at that stage would have to include so many conditions precedent (events that must occur before a loan can be advanced) that it would hardly be workable.

Amortization

Project loans typically amortize in full prior to the end of the term of the off-take agreement. In other words, tenor and amortization may deviate. Should this be the case, any outstanding amounts at maturity are payable in full at maturity. When the last payment is larger than the previous scheduled payments, it is called a balloon repayment.

As an example, let's say the tenor is five years, while the amortization is ten years, and a $1 million loan is to be repaid in four $100,000 annual payments, with a $600,000 balloon repayment due at maturity. In this case, the lenders are taking a refinancing risk, because the borrower may not be able to make such a large payment at maturity and may need to finance the repayment.

Should there be no principal payments during the term of the loan but only one payment of the whole loan amount at maturity, it is called bullet repayment. A bullet repayment, however, is an unlikely scenario within the realm of project financing.

Prepayments

If the borrower has opted for fixed interest rates, optional prepayments are usually costly. Lenders typically demand to be "made whole," meaning that the borrower will have to compensate the lender for the difference between the interest they would have earned up to maturity and the lower interest the lender will now earn, assuming a lower interest rate environment. Should interest rates have increased since financial close, the lender will not share the upside with the borrower; the interest differential will be considered zero. Additionally or alternatively, there may be prepayment penalties.

Hedging Program

Depending on circumstances and risk profile, lenders may require the borrower to submit and adhere to a hedging program with respect to commodity prices, foreign exchange or interest rates (as applicable).

Security

All assets of the project company owned at the time of loan closing, in addition to those acquired after the loan closing, will be pledged to the lenders until full repayment of the loan. This is accomplished through a general security agreement (GSA), whereby the borrower grants the lender a security interest over all current and later acquired assets, using legal documentation and registering titles against the relevant assets (where possible). Included in the assets pledged are the project company's property, accounts receivable, contractual rights and intellectual property. The lender will also ask for the parent company's shares in the project company to be pledged to the lender, mostly for some additional power in case of ongoing events of default.

When assessing the collateral's value, the lender will evaluate if the assets can be sold in a secondary market, or if they will maintain value solely in a going concern scenario (i.e., without liquidation).

Reserve Accounts

A debt service reserve account (DSRA) and major maintenance reserve account (MMRA) are almost always put in place. A DSRA typically seeks to cover six months (or up to twelve months) of scheduled debt service payments. To pay required maintenance capital expenditure, the project has to contribute, or top up, a stipulated amount to the MMRA on an annual basis, as determined by the lender's independent engineer during the due diligence investigation.

Other reserve accounts are possible, depending on the particular circumstances and risk profile. For example, as part of the first bond financing of a solar photovoltaic project in Canada, the financial structure included a degradation reserve account, which was the key to this bond issue obtaining an investment-grade rating, thereby making the issue possible. The rating agency was concerned that the performance of the solar modules installed would decline (degrade) at a higher level than anticipated and hinder the project's ability to generate the requisite returns to service its debt. Correspondingly, the financing was based on several assumptions, one of which was a linear, stable degradation of the photovoltaic solar modules. Should the modules degrade by more than 8% in any one year, however, the money in the reserve account would be made available to fix or replace them, and to reduce degradation to acceptable levels.

Priority of Application of Funds ("Project Waterfall")

At the heart of almost all project financing arrangements is a project waterfall similar to the one illustrated in Figure 13, indicating the order in which expenses are to be paid and debts repaid. Depending on the specific project and lenders, the project waterfall may have additional (reserve) accounts or other features.

All cash derived from the project, as well as amounts received under federal, state and local incentive programs, is to be held in a project cash flow account, and is typically applied in the following order, on a monthly or quarterly basis:

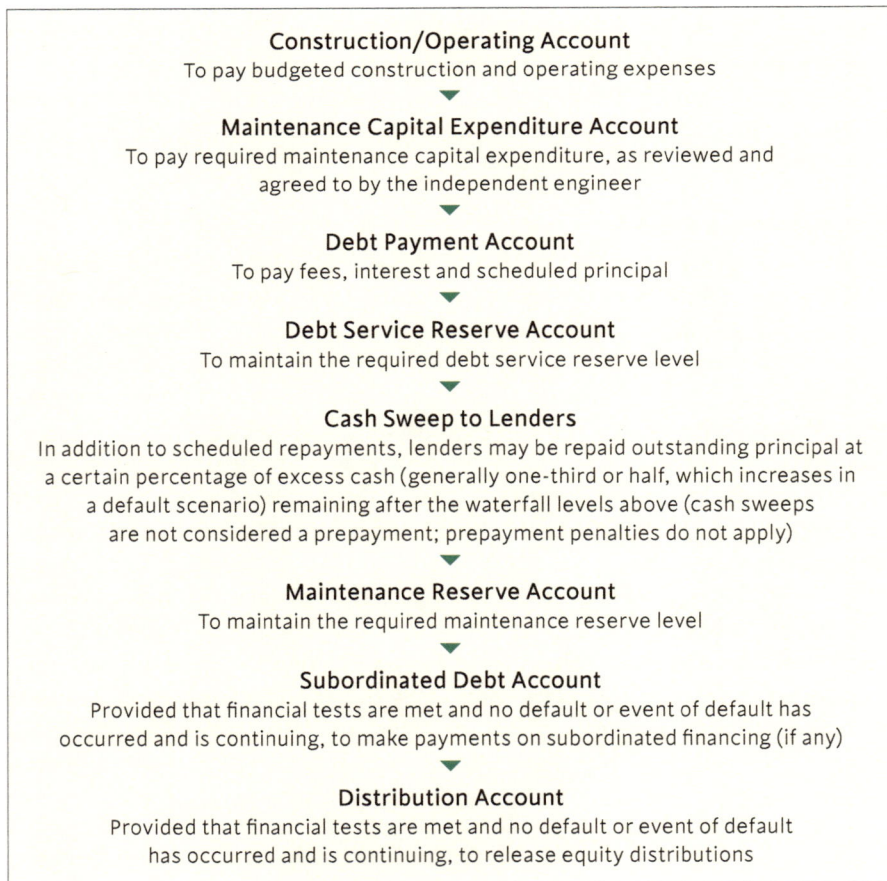

Construction/Operating Account
To pay budgeted construction and operating expenses
▼
Maintenance Capital Expenditure Account
To pay required maintenance capital expenditure, as reviewed and agreed to by the independent engineer
▼
Debt Payment Account
To pay fees, interest and scheduled principal
▼
Debt Service Reserve Account
To maintain the required debt service reserve level
▼
Cash Sweep to Lenders
In addition to scheduled repayments, lenders may be repaid outstanding principal at a certain percentage of excess cash (generally one-third or half, which increases in a default scenario) remaining after the waterfall levels above (cash sweeps are not considered a prepayment; prepayment penalties do not apply)
▼
Maintenance Reserve Account
To maintain the required maintenance reserve level
▼
Subordinated Debt Account
Provided that financial tests are met and no default or event of default has occurred and is continuing, to make payments on subordinated financing (if any)
▼
Distribution Account
Provided that financial tests are met and no default or event of default has occurred and is continuing, to release equity distributions

---

FIGURE 13: PROJECT WATERFALL

The funds in the various accounts are commonly held in escrow and controlled by the lenders.

Financial Covenants

Covenants in a loan agreement spell out what activities the borrower promises to perform (positive covenants) or to refrain from (negative covenants). They can also refer to certain balance sheet items or financial ratios that the borrower promises to stay below or above (financial covenants). Covenants help the lender to monitor the loan and the risk attached to it. Should the borrower breach any of the covenants, then the borrower is in default and the lender can take measures to deal with this situation, as stipulated in the loan agreement.

The main financial ratios a lender uses to measure a project's ability to meet debt obligations are typically the following:

Debt service coverage ratio (DSCR)	cash flow available for debt service ÷ debt service (principal, interest, fees)
Loan life coverage ratio (LLCR)	net present value of cash flow available for debt service (during the term of the debt, discounted at debt rate) ÷ outstanding debt

At the centre of the financial covenants is the DSCR, which is typically defined as EBITDA (some lenders will require deduction of necessary maintenance capital expenditures) divided by the interest and scheduled principal payments due for that period under the loan agreement. The DSCR is usually calculated on a rolling four-quarter basis, commencing 12 months after the commercial operation date (COD).

The DSCR also determines the leverage lenders are comfortable with. It is typically expected to exceed somewhere between 1.25x and 1.50x. If the project's financial model, with assumptions accepted by the lender, stipulates that the project can meet this financial covenant at the lender's maximum debt-to-total-capital ratio allowance of, say, 80%, then the lender may accept this leverage, subject to other lending criteria being met in a satisfactory manner as well.

The DSCR is regularly used as a test to determine the level of subordinated debt service and equity distributions permissible in the period of interest. Assuming the DSCR meets a predetermined threshold of, say, 1.75x and no events of default have occurred and are ongoing, the project may be allowed to distribute cash to service subordinated debt and to make equity distributions.

The LLCR is usually encountered only in larger traditional project financings. In smaller project financings, the borrower will generally encounter the DSCR and a liquidity ratio, commonly a working capital ratio (see page 73).

Addressing Probabilities ·····································

In larger project financings, the lender will require the financial model to address two or more probabilities, typically P50 and P90, and the ability to meet DSCRs in both scenarios. P50 represents the probability that the project's performance will be, on average, in the 50% confidence range; P90 represents the probability that it will be in the 90% range. A DSCR of 1.25–1.50X correlates to a P50 scenario. In a P90 scenario, required DSCR thresholds will be lower, as probability and confidence are higher.

Leverage

Leverage — the ratio of debt to total capitalization — is determined by the DSCR and other factors that make up the project's risk profile. A higher-risk profile may require 50% debt to total capitalization, while a lower-risk profile may make a ratio of 80% possible.

Furthermore, leverage is driven by the type of lender and the corresponding risk appetite. While banks are more conservative, usually not exceeding a leverage of 70–75%, life insurance companies and pension funds may be comfortable at a leverage of up to 80% or even 90%. Leasing companies providing a financial lease (see page 77) may even allow a leverage of 90–100%, depending on the quality of the asset being leased and the other lending criteria.

Looking at refinancings, in rare cases asset owners may be successful at securing debt at or above the original purchase price of the asset, benefitting from the asset's appreciation in value since acquisition. For example, a utility acquired a pumped storage asset at a discount, financing it from equity. When it went to refinance the asset a year later, an independent assessment the lenders commissioned came to the conclusion that the asset's value was now above the purchase price. Applying a suitable leverage, the lenders provided debt above the price the utility had paid. Consequently, the utility now had more money than it had originally invested, while the asset was repaying the debt. Such a wonderful outcome was, however, only possible due to the utility's strong creditworthiness.

Another, more accessible way of financing an acquisition at 100% debt goes as follows: ParentCo acquires ProjectCo for, say, $20 million. ParentCo is able to secure project financing for ProjectCo at a debt-to-equity ratio of 70% to 30%, or $14 million to $6 million. So ParentCo will have to inject $6 million in equity into ProjectCo. Assuming it has a suitable balance sheet and creditworthiness, ParentCo can raise the $6 million in the form of debt with recourse. In summary, ParentCo will have raised $14 million of project debt without recourse and $6 million of corporate debt with recourse, resulting in 100% debt financing.

Step-in Rights

Lending structures will be designed in a way that gives lenders step-in rights. This means that upon an event of default that is continuing (many events of default have cure periods), lenders have the right to take control and, hence, protect the debt. This is a crucial feature for lenders.

> ## ▶ DEFINITION
>
> **Cure Period:** The time defined in the loan agreement during which the borrower can address and clear an issue that constituted an event of default, thereby avoiding a possible termination of the agreement.

Material Adverse Change

Lenders like to incorporate a material adverse change (MAC) clause (also called a material adverse effect clause) into the loan documentation, as it covers what may not otherwise be spelled out specifically. This clause leads to the borrower being in default if an event occurs that significantly and adversely affects the borrower's ability to service the debt. The challenge for the borrower is that the loan agreement does not specify what this event might be. It can be any event that has a materially negative impact on the borrower's business. In other words, it comes down to determining materiality, or significance. Should lender and borrower disagree and take this dispute to court, the court will ultimately decide whether the event is material or not.

> **INSIDER TIP ▶** Be wary of the material adverse change clause. It is in the borrower's interest to define the events the lender may be concerned about, rather than simply accepting a MAC clause.

Restrictions

In principle, terms are structured to ensure that the cash flow the project company generates is available to service the debt. Correspondingly, the lender will place limitations on additional indebtedness, encumbrances, investments, sale of assets, consolidating or merging, creating subsidiaries, partnerships or joint ventures, servicing subordinated debt, remuneration, related party transactions and distributions. Essentially, the lender is interested in the borrower staying the same as assessed during the credit approval process, subject to certain exceptions necessary to make this workable for the borrower.

Insurance

The project company will have to maintain predetermined (and generally quite comprehensive) insurance coverage satisfactory to the lenders, as determined by the lenders' independent insurance consultant. Since warranties do not cover loss of revenues, the coverage will include business interruption insurance. All-risk insurance and third-party liability insurance are other important policies to secure.

The insurance consultant will also review the warranties and insurance coverage of the EPC provider and other material service providers, helping the lender determine the service providers' bankability.

Fees and Interest Expenses

In addition to interest rates, lenders typically request fees, such as upfront fees, due diligence fees, administration fees, monitoring fees, set-up fees and, with respect to working capital facilities, annual review fees. Furthermore, for committed but undrawn amounts, the lender will charge a commitment fee. Make sure you are clear on the total financing costs when comparing lending proposals. Also, keep in mind that the interest rate stated may not be the effective interest rate if the interest is being compounded (i.e., interest is being charged on interest).

Negative Carry and Commitment Fees • • • • • • • • • • • • • •

In bond financings, the money usually becomes available at financial close, just before the start of construction. As of that point, the issuer of the bonds (the borrower) will have to pay interest on the bonds. Until the money is required, the borrower will deposit it and earn interest — but at a lower rate than the bond rate. The difference between the issuer's interest cost and interest income is called negative carry. Considering that bond issues are generally large amounts, the negative carry can be quite substantial, which is why the project company typically includes it in the items to be financed.

In the context of this book, negative carry is not of concern, as it usually applies only to larger project financings through bond issuances. However, the term often comes up in connection with project financings.

Financial institutions typically do not make all the money available at the time of financial close, but pay it out over time as specified milestones are met. However, because these lenders make a commitment to disburse a credit subject to the fulfillment of conditions, they will usually ask for a commitment fee to be paid from the time of financial close to the time of disbursement. This fee can also represent a significant cost to the project company.

Types of Project Financiers

Figure 14 provides a simplified outline of what types of lenders currently pursue what types of project financings in Canada. Project financings have become prevalent in the renewable energy sector in Canada, which is why the table focuses on them, for illustration purposes. This outline will likely look similar in other countries. Of note is that it's not only banks but also life insurance companies and pension funds that are active project financiers.

TYPE OF PROJECT FINANCING	TYPICAL TRANSACTION SIZE	TYPES OF LENDERS IN CANADA	TERM	AMORTIZATION	COLLATERAL
Traditional infrastructure projects	>$100 million	Large Canadian banks, life insurance companies, pension funds	*Banks:* Construction plus 5–8 years *Others:* Construction plus 18 years (or longer if term of power purchase agreement is longer)	Close to the term of the offtake agreement	Limited to project
Large renewable energy projects	>$50 million	European banks, Japanese banks, traditional Canadian project financiers	*Banks:* Construction plus 5–8 years *Others:* Construction plus 18 years (or longer if term of power purchase agreement is longer)	Close to the term of the offtake agreement	Limited to project
Medium-sized renewable energy projects	>$10–20 million	Banks, life insurance companies, pension funds	*Banks:* Construction plus 5–8 years *Others:* Construction plus 18 years (or longer if term of power purchase agreement is longer)	Close to the term of the offtake agreement	Project; banks may demand (limited) corporate guarantee
Small renewable energy projects	>$5–10 million	Some banks, life insurance companies, pension funds	*Banks:* Construction plus 5–8 years *Others:* Construction plus 18 years (or longer if term of power purchase agreement is longer)	Close to the term of the offtake agreement	Project; banks may demand (limited) corporate guarantee
Very small projects	>$250,000	Commercial banking groups at banks, credit unions	5 years; possibly longer with mortgage	7–10 years; possibly longer with mortgage	Project; corporate and/or personal guarantees required; first mortgage

FIGURE 14: TYPES OF PROJECT FINANCIERS

Project Scale-up Paths and Risks

Outlined in Figure 15 are the two principal paths to project scale-up, with their different risk profiles and ease of project financing:

1. Contiguous Expansion Model

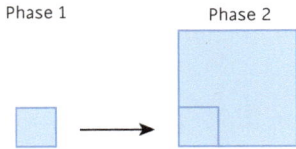

Harder to project-finance

Phase 1   Phase 2

Example: Scale-up requires expansion from, say, 30 million to 150 million litres, and the design necessitates a completely new plant.

2a. Series Expansion Model
"LOW" dollar: +/− $5 million per plant

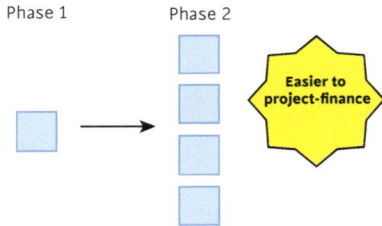

Phase 1   Phase 2

Easier to project-finance

Example: Project scales up in series from, say, 30 million litres to multiples thereof. The individual plant is of a modest cost (e.g., $1–10 million/plant).

2b. Series Expansion Model
"HIGH" dollar: +/− $20 million per plant

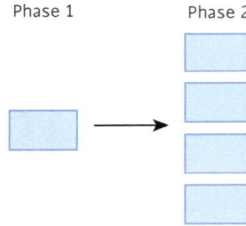

Phase 1   Phase 2

Example: Project scales up in series or in parallel from, say, 50 million litres to multiples thereof. The individual plant is of higher cost (e.g., $20 million/plant).

FIGURE 15: DIFFERENT PROJECT SCALE-UP PATHS AND RISKS

Source: WRTharp — The Climate Change Infrastructure Corporation. Used with permission.

The contiguous expansion model poses the higher risk. Expanding an existing, albeit proven, plant in size by designing a completely new plant (contiguous expansion) is much more challenging than building several already proven plants of the same smaller size (series expansion). Consequently, it is more difficult to secure financing for a contiguous expansion. Also, in principle, the expansion of smaller plants in series is easier to project-finance than the expansion of larger plants in series.

Project Financing of a Proven Concept

Pipeline of Solar Photovoltaic Rooftop Projects Raising Project Financing

Total capital expenditures:	$6.5 million
Development costs included?	Yes
Profit margin included?	Yes
Transaction costs included?	Yes
Equity:	20% = $1.3 million
Project financing (non-recourse):	80% = $5.2 million
Term:	15 years, post-COD
Repayment:	Monthly installments over 15 years
Interest rate:	6.25% per annum fixed for the term (spread is in the 350 basis point range, over Government of Canada bonds)
Lender's fees:	Due diligence fee of $25,000 and upfront fee of 1% ($65,000)
Lender's expenses:	$100,000–150,000 for due diligence investigation and legals
Security:	GSA, pledge of shares in project company
Financial covenants:	• DSCR: >1.3x • Minimum working capital • Debt and maintenance reserve accounts
Main benefit for project:	Non-recourse

When talking with solar photovoltaic project developers or EPC providers who also develop their own projects, I often learn that they do not include their development costs or profit margin in total capital expenditures. This means they exclude these items from debt financing. However, a lender will finance profit margin and hard development costs, provided they measure up to an arm's length comparison. A lender will typically also finance transaction costs, such as lender's fees, legal costs, and monies to be deposited in reserve accounts. Make sure you include these items in total project costs.

Project Financing of an Unproven Concept

Biodiesel Project in the Caribbean Raising Project Financing

Total capital expenditures:	$25 million
Development costs included?	Yes
Equity:	50% = $12.5 million ($9 million of which to be raised; $3.5 million already invested)
Project financing (non-recourse):	50% = $12.5 million (all of which to be raised)
Crucial for success:	• Technology:

- Technology:
    - Pilot plant/proof of concept
    - Proven technology with off-the-shelf parts, experienced vendor
    - Vendor financing ("skin in the game")
    - Vendor will be O&M provider
    - Satisfactory review by independent engineer
- Solid offtake agreement(s) for produced biodiesel
- 50% equity
- Reserve accounts

Biodiesel technology is not as prevalent as other renewable energy technologies, such as wind turbines or solar modules, and many biodiesel technology manufacturers are currently experiencing weak balance sheets. Correspondingly, it seems opportune to address the weaknesses of the biodiesel project by starting with a much smaller pilot plant, which will also prove the concept. The pilot plant will have to be financed from equity. The technology the client has chosen has been deployed before, documenting solid operational performance. Also, the parts used are predominantly off-the-shelf items. The experienced vendor will provide vendor financing and O&M services. This increases the vendor's motivation to deliver a solid product. The technology, along with the forecast output, will be reviewed by an independent engineer. All this, in addition to there being offtake agreements with creditworthy parties, adequate reserve accounts and equity of 50% of total capital expenditure, will provide lenders with the comfort they require.

Corporate Financing

The main difference between project financing and corporate financing is recourse. Corporate financing is recourse financing; it is based on the strength of the borrower's balance sheet, which, in turn, is affected by the borrower's financial performance (cash flow to service debt, and retained earnings to strengthen the balance sheet). In a corporate financing scenario, lenders base their assessment of the borrower's creditworthiness primarily on the company's *historical* performance. No matter how rosy the future of the business may be, if its historical financial performance does not prove that the company is on track, corporate lenders will rarely be willing to provide any funds. In contrast, lenders to a project company make their decision mainly based on the project's *future* cash flows.

With project financings, the main terms and conditions are somewhat similar across the board. For corporate financings, however, they can vary more, as they will be tailored to the specific borrower; its financial history, subsidiaries, industry and outlook; and the collateral that is available.

Types of Corporate Loans

Corporate loans can have a fixed repayment schedule or they can be revolving. They can be repayable on demand (this applies only to short-term loans) or committed for a certain period of time. They can be secured or unsecured. Lenders can advance loans in the form of cash or by providing their good name (letters of credit). Loans can also be differentiated by their use, with working capital requirements and capital expenditures being the prime uses (others are buyouts, acquisitions, start-ups, etc.).

DIFFERENTIATOR	TYPE OF LOAN	
Repayment	Installment credit with fixed repayment schedule	Revolving
Expiry	Repayable on demand (applies only to short-term loans)	Committed
Security	Secured	Unsecured
Term	Short-term	Long-term
"Currency"	Cash	Lender's good name (letter of credit)
Use	Working capital (growth)	Capital expenditure (expansion)

FIGURE 16: TYPES OF CORPORATE FINANCING LOANS

Selected Key Terms and Conditions

Following are some terms and conditions a borrower of a corporate loan should be aware of. These are in addition to type of financing and use of proceeds, borrower and sponsor, tenor, priority of funding, amortization, prepayments, hedging program, security, leverage, material adverse change, restrictions, insurance, and fees and expenses, as described in the Project Financing section (pages 58–66).

Financial Covenants

Financial covenants vary widely. However, lenders typically ask for one pertaining to the borrower's balance sheet and one regarding the borrower's performance, usually with respect to the borrower's ability to service the debt. In addition, especially in the case of working capital facilities, lenders may ask for a liquidity ratio.

In the formulas in Figure 17, "equity" or "shareholder's equity" means:

share capital + retained earnings + loans/advances granted by the shareholders and subordinated to the lender + subordinated financing − loans/advances granted to the shareholders/executives/related or arm's length companies

If there are intangible assets on the borrower's balance sheet or assets not related to the operation of the business, the lender may choose to work with tangible net worth or tangible equity, deducting intangible items from equity:

tangible net worth (or tangible equity) = equity as defined above − intangible assets − assets not related to the operations of the business

Intangible assets may include intellectual property (patents, trademarks, copyrights), goodwill and brand recognition.

Debt may be comprised of all short- and long-term debt, or the lender may prefer for it to just include all long-term debt.

Note that the financial covenants' thresholds, which the borrower promises to stay below or above, are based on the borrower's financial projections in a way that seems reasonable. If the covenants do not appear achievable or there is hardly any room for error, the lender will be open to adjusting them during the

> **INSIDER TIP ▶** Make sure the financial covenants you and your lender define in the loan agreement are achievable. It is acceptable to ask for a bit of wiggle room, as neither the lender nor you wants the covenants to be triggered easily.

loan negotiation process. Nobody is served if covenants are too aggressive and the borrower breaches them soon after the loan is advanced. Financial covenants can also be structured, meaning that the parties can agree to a profile where the threshold decreases or increases, as applicable, over time.

BALANCE SHEET COVENANTS	
Debt to total capitalization (leverage)	debt ÷ (debt + equity)
Debt to equity	debt ÷ equity
Shareholders' equity	expressed as a minimum dollar amount
Tangible net worth	total assets − liabilities − intangible assets (expressed as a minimum dollar amount)
PERFORMANCE COVENANTS	
Interest coverage ratio	EBITDA ÷ interest
Debt service coverage ratio	EBITDA ÷ (principal + interest)
Hybrid	debt ÷ EBITDA
LIQUIDITY RATIOS	
Liquid ratio (indicates the company's ability to use its near cash to cover its current liabilities immediately)	liquid assets (cash + cash equivalents + marketable securities + accounts receivable) ÷ current liabilities
Working capital ratio (indicates whether the business has ample working capital; i.e., the excess of current liabilities over current assets used to meet short-term obligations, quickly take advantage of opportunities and qualify for favourable credit terms)	current assets ÷ current liabilities (due within the next 12 months)

FIGURE 17: FINANCIAL COVENANTS

Most Favoured Nations Clause

Where a borrower has various lending relationships, the new lender may ask for a "most favoured nations clause." This means that, if the borrower concedes beneficial terms to one lender, the borrower will have to make these terms available to all lenders. In general, this a reasonable request.

Cross Default

Cross default is a standard term that puts the borrower in default under the loan agreement when the borrower defaults on another obligation that is not covered by the loan agreement.

Corporate Financing

*Municipal Energy Distribution Company Securing a Term Loan
for Capital Expenditures*

Size of line of credit:	$10 million
Term:	3 years
Repayment:	Monthly installments with balloon repayment at maturity
Interest rate:	Lender's cost of funds plus a margin of less than 1% per annum, fixed
Lender's fees:	Upfront fee of $10,000
Security:	GSA, first ranking
Financial covenants:	• DSCR: >1.25x • Debt to EBITDA: <2.5x

This case study is an example of a straightforward transaction due to the borrower's low risk profile, the solid nature of the collateral and the medium-length term of the transaction.

Corporate Financing in Preparation for Project Financing

Company with Small Wind Projects in the UK Raising Recourse Financing as Proof of Concept in Preparation of Much Larger Project Financing Raise

Total capital expenditures:	$11 million
Development costs included?	Yes
Profit margin included?	Yes
Equity:	37% = $4 million
Senior debt financing (recourse):	63% = $7 million
Term:	5 years, post-COD
Repayment:	Monthly installments with balloon repayment at maturity
Interest rate:	Approximately 7.0% per annum floating (variable); company borrowed in Great Britain pounds at 1-month London Interbank Offered Rate of about 0.5% per annum at closing, plus a margin of 6.5% per annum
Lender's fees:	$35,000 (0.5%)
Security (borrower):	GSA
Security (sponsor):	Guarantee, GSA subordinated to senior lender of line of credit, pledge of shares in the borrower
Financial covenants:	• Working capital ratio: >1.25x • DSCR: >1.5x • Debt to EBITDA: <2.5x
Main benefit for borrower and sponsor:	Groundwork for much larger project financing of young sponsor

A client who manufactures small wind turbines decided to not only sell its products to project developers in the United Kingdom but also develop its own UK projects under the local feed-in tariff program. This wind manufacturer has enjoyed tremendous growth over the last few years and, by the time it was looking for debt financing of its UK projects, its turbines had been operational for more than two years, showing a solid performance record. That said, the manufacturer had only recently turned cash-flow positive, largely due to the steep growth rate. Because of this, lenders were not ready to provide project financing quite yet. Accordingly, we helped the company secure a relatively small loan of $7 million, which is backed by the parent company through a guarantee. This successful proof of concept is now instrumental in establishing a much larger project financing facility for the company's project rollout.

Loan Syndication

Lenders prefer sharing the risk of larger loans through loan syndication, where the loan is provided by a group of lenders, each of whom contributes a portion of the total loan. The lender (or lenders) with the role of "arranger" structures and arranges the loan; the "agent" administers it. There are three types of syndication deals: underwritten deals, best-efforts deals and club deals.

Underwritten Deals

In this case, the arranger underwrites the whole loan — or, in other words, guarantees the entire commitment. For this, the arranger receives an underwriting fee on top of the arrangement fee. Offering an underwritten deal also provides the arranger with a competitive advantage, helping it win the mandate. The borrower benefits from having certainty that the loan will get placed.

Once the loan is underwritten, the underwriter syndicates it. The underwriter must absorb any amounts it cannot place, at least for the time being, but will try to sell the paper later, when market conditions have improved, possibly at a discount to reduce its exposure.

INSIDER TIP ▶ When agreeing to an underwritten deal, beware of flex-language that provides the underwriter with an out should market conditions or other criteria change.

Best-Efforts Deals

Under this arrangement, the arranger agrees to exercise its best efforts to place the whole loan. However, it guarantees only the portion of the loan it is likely to finance personally. Should the loan end up being undersubscribed, the borrower may be forced to accept a lower loan amount, or the loan agreement may be cancelled entirely.

Club Deals

In a club deal, the individual lenders deal directly with the borrower and with each other. The arranger does not lead the transaction but is rather first among equals. Correspondingly, each syndication partner receives the same share, or nearly the same share, of the fees. This type of syndication is typically done for smaller transactions, perhaps starting at around $20 million, and with only a few lenders.

Financial Lease

A financial lease, also called a capital lease, is geared towards raising finances to pay for assets. It is not a genuine rental but a commercial arrangement whereby the lessee (user of the asset) will select an asset and the lessor (finance company) will purchase that asset. The financial lease tends to extend over most of the economic life of the leased equipment. It is generally non-cancellable, providing certainty to the parties. While the lessor is the legal owner of the asset, the lessee will have use of that asset during the lease. The lease payments the lessee will make are fixed obligations equivalent to debt service. From a tax perspective, since the lessee does not own the asset, it cannot depreciate it. On the other hand, lease payments are fully tax-deductible.

Financial leases can be structured in different ways but, principally, the lessee will be responsible for the asset's maintenance, insurance and operating expenses. The lessee also faces the risks and receives the rewards of ownership. If the asset turns out to be more costly and less suitable than anticipated, the lessee will have to bear the consequences. If it turns out to be a great success, the profit goes to the lessee, not the lessor. Financial leases are usually structured so that the lessee can acquire the asset at maturity.

In many respects, a financial lease is equivalent to a secured loan. The lessee must make a series of fixed payments. If the lessee fails to do so, the lessor can repossess the asset. That said, there are two qualifications to be pointed out. First, at financial lease expiry, the lessor, as legal owner, gets the residual value of the asset; once a secured loan is paid off, the user owns the asset free and clear. Secondly, lessors and secured creditors may be treated differently in bankruptcy. If the bankruptcy court decides that the leased asset is "essential" to the lessee's business, it "affirms" the lease. The bankrupt company can continue to use the asset, but it must also continue to make the lease payments. This can be good news for the lessor: it is paid cash, while even secured creditors are not paid until the bankruptcy process has worked itself out. If the lease is "rejected," the lessor can, of course, recover the leased asset. If it is worth less than the future payments the lessee had promised, the lessor can try to recoup this loss. However, the lessor will have to get in line with the unsecured creditors.

Another financial lease construct that provides the user with liquidity is a "sale and lease-back" arrangement. Here, the lessor purchases an asset the user (lessee) has on its books (such as a machine or other larger equipment) and then leases it back to the lessee.

Make note of the fact, however, that lease accounting is being reviewed. A reform is under way that aims to see the net present value of a company's future lease payments reflected on its balance sheet as a liability.

CHAPTER FOUR

SUBORDINATE FINANCING

What Is Subordinate Financing?

Subordinate financing is an investment made in the form of debt. In other words, it is debt financing that has equity characteristics. Not everyone is on the same page when it comes to defining the various terms of this hybrid instrument. In the context of this book, subordinate financing covers sub debt (which looks more like debt) and mezzanine debt (which looks more like equity). Other common terms for subordinate financing are "quasi-equity," "junior debt" and "structured equity."

Subordinate financing has the following characteristics:

- It consists of a committed, long-term facility.
- The borrower has the obligation to repay the loan according to a predetermined schedule, like regular debt financing. However, the repayment is flexible, structured to match future cash flows.
- The loan is subordinated to senior debt, which consists of the borrower's term loans and/or working capital facilities. This means that security and debt service rank behind the senior lender.
- The size of the loan that is acceptable to the financier is primarily determined by the borrower's historical cash flows, not by the borrower's capitalization. In other words, it is not leverage but a form of company valuation that establishes the loan size. As an indication, the loan tends to be 1–2x the borrower's normalized EBITDA. This approach resembles equity financing.
- The return comes from scheduled interest payments (a debt characteristic) and some sort of kicker (a variable component), such as warrants to purchase shares in the borrower at a discount, royalties on revenues or EBITDA, or bonus payments on the borrower's equity value or EBITDA. Through these kickers, the financier has the opportunity to participate in the borrower's upside (an equity characteristic).

Subordinate Financing Application

This type of financing is typically used in the context of ownership changes (management buyouts), acquisitions (leveraged buyouts) and where growth or expansion capital is required. Subordinate financing comes into play where conventional financing is unavailable or limited, or as an alternative to equity.

Sub Debt

Sub debt is typically structured more like a debt instrument, with monthly or quarterly installments, and possibly one larger principal payment (balloon) at maturity. The interest rate tends to be in the range of 11–15% per annum. The variable component that allows the lender to participate in the borrower's upside can be negotiated in various forms, as outlined above.

Mezzanine Debt

Mezzanine debt is usually structured more like equity, with a bullet repayment at maturity. The interest rate may be lower, as more emphasis is put on the variable component: the upside opportunity.

Selected Key Terms and Conditions

The borrower will be faced with similar terms and conditions as outlined in Chapter Three. The terms and conditions of specific interest with respect to this unique financing instrument are discussed here.

The financial covenants usually encountered in subordinate financing transactions are:

- Minimum working capital ratio;
- Maximum term debt-to-equity ratio, whereby sub debt tends to be considered debt;
- Minimum available funds threshold;
- Minimum tangible net worth threshold.

Goodwill (the purchase price for a company minus the company's book value) is usually not deducted for subordinate financing purposes, as the subordinate finance lender believes it has value and, hence, lends against it.

Quite frequently, the loan agreement will stipulate an annual cash flow sweep, whereby a certain amount (typically 25–50%) of the borrower's surplus cash flow (as determined by the borrower's most recent audited financial statements) is applied against the outstanding balance of the loan within, say, 90 days of fiscal year-end.

All shareholder loans must be subordinated to the loan. The shareholders who are also on the management team may have to provide a conditional guarantee ensuring that they will devote their time, expertise and ability to the borrower's business and keep their existing ownership stakes in the borrower. Payments under the conditional guarantee will usually only take effect upon specific events, such as fraud, negligence or misappropriation of funds.

For collateral, the financier will request a general security agreement (GSA) over all fixed and floating assets, subordinated to the senior lenders.

To ensure working capital is sufficient, the subordinate finance lender will typically request that the borrower maintain a working capital facility.

Subordination and Postponement Agreement

Also called an intercreditor agreement, priority agreement or tripartite agreement (as it involves three (or more) parties: the borrower, the senior lender and the junior lender), a comprehensive subordination and postponement agreement stipulates the following:

- Postponement and subordination of the subordinate financing (SubFin) security to the senior financing (SeniorFin) security to the extent of the borrower's indebtedness to the senior lender, including the debt obligations plus all accrued interest and expenses incurred by the senior lender (senior lender obligations).
- SubFin security and SeniorFin security to rank in descending order of priority as follows:
  - First, the SeniorFin security to the extent of the senior lender obligations;
  - Second, the SubFin security to the extent of the SubFin obligations;
  - Third, the SeniorFin security in excess of the senior lender obligations;
  - Fourth, the SubFin security in excess of the SubFin obligations.
- Until the senior lender obligations have been paid in full, the SubFin lender shall not require the borrower to make any payments towards the SubFin obligations other than scheduled principal and interest payments and cash flow sweeps, as specifically agreed upon.
- Any default with respect to the SubFin loan agreement will be an event of default under the SeniorFin loan agreement.
- Defaults are often divided into significant defaults (default in payment of principal and interest or any financial covenant) and material defaults (all defaults that are not significant).
- Following the occurrence of a default, the SubFin lender shall not receive any payments (in financing terms, the SubFin lender shall stand still) until the earliest of the following events or dates has occurred:
  - A certain amount of time has passed, with this time being longer with respect to a significant default (perhaps 90–150 days) and shorter regarding a material default (60–120 days);
  - The default is cured;
  - The SeniorFin lender has taken steps to enforce the SeniorFin security;
  - All indebtedness to the SeniorFin lender has been repaid.
- It is usually agreed that there will be a maximum of one such payment standstill in any consecutive 12-month period.

Senior lenders consider subordinate financing to be equity when it is "deeply subordinated." This is accomplished when the subordination and postponement agreement is drafted comprehensively along the criteria outlined above.

Lighter versions may not incorporate standstill periods or differentiate between significant and material defaults. Some lighter versions may not provide any details on the ranking of payments during the ordinary course of business or in case of defaults; they may simply outline the ranking of payments following the lenders' enforcement of security interests.

INSIDER TIP ▶ For a senior lender to accept subordinate financing as equity, the subordinated financing will have to be "deeply subordinated" to the senior debt.

The Benefits of Subordinate Financing

Subordinate financing has the following benefits:

- It offers a range of customized financing structures designed to provide sufficient residual cash flow for growth during the term of the investment.
- It allows for an investment in intangible assets, making debt financing possible where there are no hard assets available to serve as security.
- It is treated as equity by senior lenders (subject to its deep subordination), which also improves financial ratios and creates leverage with senior lenders.

In addition, subordinate financing has the following advantages over equity financing:

- It limits shareholder dilution.
- It takes less control.
- It is less expensive.
- It is a more tax-effective instrument, as interest is tax-deductible.
- It offers more flexibility in light of a customized repayment schedule.
- It requires no shareholder agreement.

Subordinate Financing

Marketing Communications Company Raising Subordinate Financing

Type of transaction:	$1.5 million in working capital to support high sales growth
Rationale for sub debt vs. senior debt:	No material assets; senior debt at its maximum at $2 million
Selected financial info:	• Sales: $8 million • Normalized EBITDA: $2 million • Fixed assets (book value): $0.5 million
Term:	3.5 years
Repayment:	Monthly installments with a balloon of 30% of loan amount at maturity
Interest rate:	12% per annum, fixed
Additional return:	1.75% of EBITDA
Targeted return:	18% per annum
Lender's fees:	Small annual administration fee of $500
Security:	GSA with priority to senior loan
Financial covenants:	• Minimum working capital ratio • Maximum term debt-to-equity ratio
Main benefit for borrower:	Raised funds without dilution at a cost below private equity; sales growth above internally sustainable levels
Main benefit for senior lender:	Fully secured by strong (and growing) current asset coverage

This marketing communications company was experiencing tremendous growth. Its senior debt facility was maxed out at $2 million. Through sub debt, the company was able to attract additional funds of $1.5 million, based not on its insufficient assets, but on its cash flow (normalized annual EBITDA was $2 million). The company accomplished this without diluting its capital, at a cost below private equity. The senior lender, enjoying first ranking, welcomed the sub debt, as its collateral (accounts receivable) increased with the borrower's growth.

Convertible Debentures as a Form of Subordinate Financing

For companies that have a higher risk profile (because of their stage of development or the sector they are in) but also attractive growth potential, a convertible debenture may be a good financing option. A convertible debenture is a bond that the holder can convert into a specified number of common or preferred shares in the issuing company at a predetermined event or date. It is a security with debt- and equity-like characteristics.

> ▶ **DEFINITION**
>
> **Coupon Rate:** The interest rate of a security.

In light of the upside opportunity, a convertible bond may have a lower coupon rate than non-convertible debt. The purchaser of the bond protects the downside through receipt of interest payments and return of the principal at maturity. The issuer of the bond enjoys the benefit of reduced interest payments and, if the bond is converted into equity, disappearance of the debt. Upon conversion, however, shareholders' equity will be diluted.

If a company believes its present share price is undervalued and, correspondingly, it prefers not to issue any shares at the current time, a convertible debenture might be an attractive fundraising option. The company could structure the convertible debenture so that its conversion price is above the current stock price, possibly increasing every year.

With respect to ranking, convertible debentures rank ahead of the underlying equity of the issuer and are therefore less risky than the underlying equity. Senior lenders will request that convertible debentures be subordinated, and subordinate lenders usually will too. That said, a convertible debenture is not automatically subordinated. It is possible for a convertible debenture to have a senior or *pari passu* (equal) ranking.

As a safeguard, convertible debentures tend to concede a call option to the issuer, giving the issuer the right to redeem the debenture prior to maturity, at the call price. This allows the issuer to take advantage of a refinancing at a lower interest rate; it may also give the issuer the required power to force a conversion into shares.

> **INSIDER TIP ▶** Beware of convertible debentures in the earlier stages of a company's development.

Convertible debentures are often structured in such a way that, upon the occurrence of an event of default, all monies owed pursuant to the convertible debenture become due and payable. As the issuer may not have the means to pay those monies, the bond holder may be able to force a conversion into shares at more favourable terms, which can, in some cases, lead to the existing shareholders losing control of the company. This scenario is especially likely to play out with emerging companies, as defaults can happen more easily in the start-up stage.

Vendor Financing as a Form of Subordinate Financing

Vendor financing is a loan provided by the vendor (current owner and seller) of shares or assets. Instead of the buyer raising the equivalent of the required purchase price, the vendor may be prepared to provide a loan for part of it. Essentially, the vendor defers the payment.

Vendor financing can have as many different structures as vendor and purchaser (or borrower) come up with and agree on. For example, the vendor may provide a five-year loan with a holiday on principal payments for the first one or two years. The loan could be structured so that it is fully repaid by, say, the end of five years. Alternatively, vendor and purchaser may agree on smaller installments, leaving a larger amount to be paid at maturity. Should the purchaser not be able to make the payments, the loan could convert into equity at a predetermined value. Or, if the asset being financed is tangible, it could be returned to the vendor at a predetermined pricing formula, in consideration of the vendor's efforts and the asset's depreciation.

Interest rates for vendor financings tend to be reasonable — comparable to bank rates —because the vendor understands the risks of the shares or assets being sold, and because the vendor generates a profit through the sale itself. The interest charged, however, will exceed the vendor's financing costs.

CHAPTER FIVE

THE MECHANICS OF A FINANCING TRANSACTION

This chapter moves away from theory to delve into the practical tasks involved in pursuing a financing transaction. Your first step will be deciding which financing route or combination of routes to pursue. Once you have a game plan in mind, you will need to make an effective fundraising pitch to persuade financiers to come onboard. You will then need to prepare yourself for the due diligence investigation that will be performed by each of the financiers you approach. The financiers will also carry out return calculations, with certain return expectations in mind. The financing transaction will have to be of suitable quality, but it will also have to meet or exceed certain return thresholds for a financier to provide the funds. Finally, you will have to wait through the financiers' decision-making process, providing them with information and documentation and negotiating details as needed.

In this chapter, you will find all the information you need to prepare yourself for each step along the road to successfully acquiring financing so you can pursue your company's goals.

> **INSIDER TIP** ▶ Secure as much debt as is prudent and complement it with as little equity as necessary, while maintaining a suitable equity cushion for rainy days.

Deciding Which Financing Routes to Pursue

How do you decide whether to seek out equity financing, debt financing (whether project financing or corporate financing), subordinate financing or some combination of the three? The short answer is: choose those instruments and combinations that keep your weighted average cost of capital as low as possible. Debt has the lowest cost of capital and equity has the highest, while subordinate financing sits somewhere in between the two. Subordinate financing may allow you to raise debt where senior debt is exhausted, or it may enable you to substitute some of the required equity. Of course, monetary considerations alone are not going to lead to success. You also need to make sure you maintain a suitable equity cushion for rainy days. Consequently, the best strategy is to secure as much debt as possible and complement it with as little equity as necessary, while keeping equity at levels that allow the company to withstand temporary business setbacks.

As you consider your options, it may help to look at various points of comparison for each type of financing:

- **Focus:** A financier will evaluate an opportunity from different angles depending on the financial instrument. An equity investor will assess the company's growth potential and future cash flow. A project financier is also interested in future cash flows, while a corporate lender's primary focus is on the historical performance of the business in question, as well as the assets available to serve as collateral. A financier providing subordinate financing will want to determine the enterprise value and, hence, will need to understand the company's historical cash flows. Do you see the strengths of your business mostly in the future, or in your past and future?
- **Criteria driving the size of the financial instrument:** Different financial instruments rely on different criteria to determine the level of the financier's involvement. Equity financing and subordinate financing are driven by EBITDA multiples. With debt financing, senior lenders determine the level of debt they are comfortable advancing, with the help of leverage and DSCR. What criteria will result in the largest financing for your company?
- **Security:** Equity investments are not secured. Debt financing requires first ranking security. Subordinate financing usually takes collateral but will subordinate it to senior lenders. What type of security do you have or want to make available?
- **Return:** The business will have to pay equity investors dividends (if possible) and allow them to participate in its upside. Lenders are paid interest. Subordinate financiers receive interest payments in addition to their participation in the business's upside. What type of return are you comfortable paying?
- **Return expectations and risk:** As discussed further on page 97, different financiers have varying return expectations that go hand and hand with perceived risks. The higher the risks, the higher the return expectations. Correspondingly, equity investors have the highest return expectations, then subordinate financiers, then senior lenders. What level of returns are you prepared to pay?
- **Due diligence and monitoring:** The level of risk also determines the extent of a financier's due diligence and monitoring. The due diligence investigation and monitoring of an equity investor (especially in the case of a financial investor) will typically be more involved than those of a subordinate financier, project lender or corporate lender (in that order). What level of due diligence investigation and monitoring are you comfortable with?
- **Involvement of financier:** Equity investors tend to be more hands-on, while subordinate financiers and senior lenders are usually passive. What level of involvement do you find helpful or acceptable?

Figure 18 gives a simplified overview of the various forms of financing, to facilitate the comparison just outlined.

	EQUITY FINANCING	DEBT FINANCING		SUBORDINATE FINANCING
		Project Financing	Corporate Financing	
Focus	Growth potential; future cash flows	Future cash flows	Historical performance; assets	Enterprise value (historical cash flows)
Criteria driving the size of the financial instrument	(Comparable) EBITDA multiple	DSCR; leverage	DSCR; leverage	1–2× normalized EBITDA
Security	n/a	1st ranking	1st ranking	Subordinated
Return	Dividends and upside	Interest	Interest	Interest and upside
Return expectations	Very high (>25% IRR)	Moderate	Moderate	High (17–23% IRR)
Risk	Very high	Moderate	Low to moderate	High
Due diligence and monitoring	Very high	Medium to high	Low to medium	High
Involvement of financer	Active	Passive	Passive	Minimal/passive

FIGURE 18: FINANCING SUMMARY

The Pitch

When presenting the investment or lending opportunity, it is crucial to be transparent and knowledgeable about the benefits to the financier (i.e., have the answer to: "What's in it for me?"), as well as the risks. To make sure you fully understand the risks, it is best to conduct a due diligence investigation yourself beforehand, to uncover any holes (see page 93 for more information on due diligence). You can then determine whether you can fix them. If not, address them openly and up front, and give the financier your view on how the risks can be mitigated. That creates trust. There is no benefit in hiding anything, as financiers will come across all the holes eventually, with the possible consequence that they will lose trust and walk away.

The financier may require third-party verification of assumptions and markets, and will typically want to choose the independent consultant that will provide those verifications. You may wish to obtain reports from independent consultants beforehand, to attract financiers. If so, make sure to select well-known, reputable service providers you know financiers trust so that the financier will accept those reports and not require additional ones, resulting in material costs.

A warm introduction (through a reputable referral source) is a lot more effective than a cold call. Lenders in particular prefer originating opportunities through their own network. They will treat somebody who cold-calls them with a bit more suspicion. If possible, network yourself to the financier so that you can take advantage of a warm introduction.

When contacting financiers, make sure you are equipped with a short overview (a "teaser"), a presentation and all the necessary documents in a virtual data room. You will want to have prepared a nondisclosure and confidentiality agreement so you can share it with interested parties right away, without any delays.

The feedback you receive from the potential financiers may be valuable. Be flexible and adjust your approach and documentation to reflect relevant comments. This may turn into an iterative process, but don't shy away from it, as it will likely result in a stronger, optimized pitch.

Teaser

The teaser is a one- to two-page overview of the investment or lending opportunity, outlining the company or project and the investment/lending highlights. It focuses on the benefits for the financier. The teaser does not need to discuss the risks.

The teaser helps financiers decide whether they want to learn more about the opportunity. It allows a simple yes or no screening.

Presentation

Financiers who decide to hear more about the opportunity after reviewing the teaser will expect additional information to be presented in the form of a PowerPoint slide deck. The presentation should be no longer than about 20 minutes. The financier is still screening the opportunity. While the teaser will get you a foot in the door, the presentation may allow you to step into the foyer. It should be no more than 10 to 15 slides, though more slides can be put in the appendix for the financier's later perusal.

It is important that financiers understand early on what you are asking of them. Do not wait until the end to share that information. People listen differently and more constructively when they know what they are being asked to do. The following is an effective way of organizing the slides:

- **Slide 1:** A brief introduction to the company or project.
- **Slide 2:** The investment or lending highlights. (What's in it for them?)
- **Slide 3:** Details about what you are asking of the financier.
- **Further slides:** More information on the company/project; a description of the management team; major points of the due diligence checklist. (Address this last item without going too deep. The business plan and other documents in the data room will provide a deeper level of detail once the financier has decided to pursue your opportunity.)

> ▶ **DEFINITION**
>
> **Financial Model:** A number of spreadsheets (usually created in Excel) presenting all assumptions (inputs) and outputs with respect to a project for the life of the project, or with respect to a business typically for the next three to five years. It includes projected profit and loss, a cash flow statement and a balance sheet for the chosen timeframe, as well as return calculations and, if applicable, payback periods for the investment.

Financial Model

The financial model is a crucial screening tool for both investors and project lenders, as both investment and lending decisions are materially impacted by future cash flows. Corporate financing decisions, albeit based dominantly on historical cash flows, will also take financial projections into account.

Data Room

Many data rooms contain too much information. Limit the documents you provide there to what's on the due diligence checklist. More information may be overwhelming or confusing, unless, of course, you possess material information that the due diligence checklist does not cover.

Organize the data room along the structure of the due diligence checklist. This makes it easier for the financier to work with the data room and to check on certain items.

The Due Diligence Investigation

During the due diligence investigation, the financier examines the fundraiser's business carefully to gain a full understanding of the risks involved, as well as the opportunities to mitigate those risks. If the financier is an investor, the focus of the investigation will be to determine whether the potential investee will be able to generate the expected return. If the financier is a lender, the focus of the investigation will be to determine whether the potential borrower will be able to service the debt (i.e., make the scheduled interest and principal payments).

From the Perspective of an Investor

The following are usually at the centre of the investor's due diligence program:

- The quality and breadth of the management team (especially if it is expected to stay on);
- The product's defendable market position;
- The growth prospect of the business and the market;
- Marketability and scalability;
- Exit strategy.

INSIDER TIP ▶ Conduct a due diligence investigation on your own business (possibly with the help of a financial advisor) before contacting a financier. That way, you will have a clear understanding of the risks and will be able to either mitigate them before your fundraising efforts or address them properly when speaking to the financier. This will make you look more competent and make your business look more attractive.

There are long-term investors who are not concerned about an exit within three to five years, especially those investors who invest in infrastructure projects with long-term annuity-style returns. Do not aim for the exit; aim for beyond the exit. You do not want to run out of steam by the time the exit is supposed to roll around but doesn't, due to various potential delays.

Appendix A (page 102) outlines the main areas the investor will want to understand and be comfortable with.

> ## ▶ DEFINITION
>
> **Exit Strategy:** A way for investors to monetize their investment and, hence, realize their capital gain. Examples are an initial public offering, the sale of the business, and a share buy-back by the company. Also called a "liquidity event."

From the Perspective of a Lender

At the heart of the lender's due diligence investigation are the following criteria:

- Competence;
- Cash flow;
- Collateral.

Does the management team have the knowledge and experience, the breadth and depth to bring the business to success and keep it there? Or is the success of the company tightly linked to the efforts and relationships of only one key person? Will the cash flow be sufficient to service the debt (i.e., to make the scheduled interest and principal payments)? Is there sufficient collateral to mitigate the risk, as assessed by the lender?

> **INSIDER TIP ▶** Strong collateral will not trump questionable cash flow projections.

The lender considers collateral a safety net, not a deal-maker. If the lender's assessment of the management team and/or cash flow projections does not provide the lender with the level of comfort desired, solid collateral will not convince the lender to agree to the loan. The response you can expect from a lender in this situation is: "We are not a pawn shop."

The lender will go through a lengthy due diligence investigation. The main items this investigation will cover are detailed in the checklists in Appendix B (page 104) and Appendix C (page 107). Appendix B addresses the information required for project financing; Appendix C, the information needed for corporate financing. Since the lists are general in nature, certain items may not be applicable in all cases.

In the case of subordinate financing, the borrower will have to address the information requirements listed in Appendix C and, furthermore, provide any prior valuations of the business or its assets, as well as any previous arm's length or other offer for the business or its assets.

> **INSIDER TIP ▶** The quality of the management team is an integral part of any investor and lender's due diligence investigation. For that reason, it is important for the company's head to prepare the team for what to expect and to ensure that the key team members are sufficiently skilled and committed.

Return Calculations

Financiers have at their disposal many different return calculations they can use to decide whether it is beneficial to them to provide financing to your business. In general, however, and as discussed below, investors use internal rate of return (IRR), while banks are guided by risk-adjusted return on capital (RAROC). Other lenders rely on internal spread sheets that determine targeted margins based on the internal risk rating.

Considerations of Strategic Investors

A strategic equity investor typically uses the investment opportunity's internal rate of return as a measuring stick for its attractiveness in relation to other investment opportunities the investor may be exploring. The IRR can be expressed as levered (calculated under consideration of the underlying equity and debt financing) or unlevered (assuming 100% equity financing). If an equity investor has a choice between many investment opportunities, unlevered IRR appears to be the more objective standard of comparison. Different investment opportunities can be levered to varied degrees. A project with leverage of 80% debt and 20% equity will have a higher levered IRR than a project that can only be levered at 60% debt and 40% equity. While one could argue that this benefit should be reflected in the decision-making process, it must be considered that the investor ultimately has to meet a certain overriding leverage, consolidated for the whole group of investments. If that leverage is, for example, 70% debt and 30% equity, future opportunities may have to be levered at a lower than possible ratio to balance out those investments to which the investor had already committed a higher leverage. To prevent this dilemma, sophisticated strategic investors use unlevered IRR as a measure when making an investment decision.

The IRR (or discounted cash flow rate of return) is the discount rate that makes the net present value (NPV) zero. Below is a formula that allows you to solve for the IRR in an investment project lasting "t" years, where C = cash flows in the various periods; C_0 = capital expenditure; and C_1 through C_t = cash flow from the investment project in each year.

$$NPV = C_0 + [C_1 \div (1+ IRR)] + [C_2 \div (1+ IRR)^2] + \ldots + [C_t \div (1+ IRR)^t] = 0$$

Actual calculation of an IRR usually involves trial and error, but since modern technology easily accomplishes the calculation for us, I will not go into detail here.

IRR can be expressed pre-tax or after-tax. Unless the investor enjoys tax exemption, IRR is typically calculated and compared on an after-tax basis.

Considerations of Financial Investors and Subordinate Financing Providers

Financial investors and subordinate financing providers will use levered IRR as their return criterion, as they need not concern themselves with the consolidated group leverage issues outlined above.

Basel Accords ····································

The Basel Accords are rules set by the Basel Committee on Bank Supervision, which meets in Basel, Switzerland, at the Bank for International Settlement. These rules are recommendations on banking regulations in the member countries, mainly with respect to credit risk, market risk and operational risk. The primary purpose of the Basel Accords is to ensure that banks maintain sufficient capital based on the institution's underlying credit, market and operational risks, so that they will not falter in case of unexpected losses. Currently, the member countries are: Argentina, Australia, Belgium, Brazil, Canada, China, France, Germany, Hong Kong SAR, India, Indonesia, Italy, Japan, Korea, Luxembourg, Mexico, the Netherlands, Russia, Saudi Arabia, Singapore, South Africa, Spain, Sweden, Switzerland, Turkey, the United Kingdom and the United States.

Considerations of Senior Lenders

Banks are guided by risk-adjusted return on capital, which takes into consideration the tightly regulated capital that a bank must allocate against each loan in line with its specific risk assessment. Over the last several years, the amount of this capital has increased as the Basel Accords (see box, above) have become stricter. This means that loans have become more costly for the bank and, hence, for the borrower. If the borrower provides more collateral, thereby decreasing the risk, the bank will have to allocate less capital and the borrower can reduce interest expenses. In addition, the longer the term of the financing, the more capital the bank has to allocate. This explains why banks prefer to cap their long-term lending at five to seven years.

Because pension funds and life insurance companies are subject to different regulations than banks, they apply internal risk ratings on individual financings (if not rated publicly) and then determine a spread over a reference rate (in Canada, the Government of Canada bonds with a tenor that is closest to the average life of the loan). The spread is based on where comparable rated corporate bond spreads are trading, plus a premium for the illiquid, structured nature of the investment.

Return Expectations

Return expectations go hand in hand with the risk investors or lenders are willing to expose themselves to. Correspondingly, an equity investor will have higher return expectations than a subordinate financing provider, who will have higher expectations than a senior lender. An equity investor in a start-up opportunity will require higher returns (>30% levered IRR) than an equity investor in a solid infrastructure project with long-term annuity-style returns (≥12% levered IRR). Furthermore, while lenders are driven by the interest they earn in relation to the risk, investors are driven by the upside they believe in. Subordinate financing providers consider both aspects.

Bank spreads are dependent on the type of loan, the risk of the borrower and the form of transaction. They start as low as a few basis points and can go as high as several hundred basis points. To offer an indication of risk and return expectations, Figure 19 (page 98) illustrates the long-term financing of a typical wind or solar project.

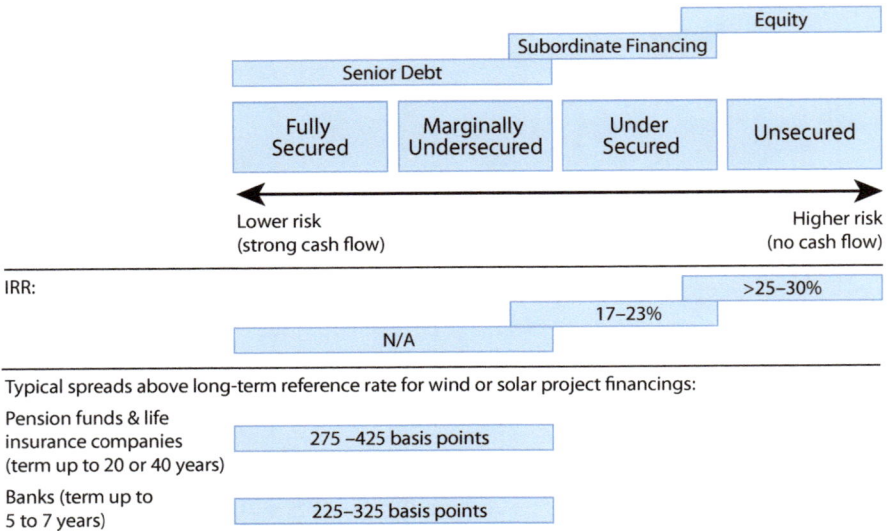

FIGURE 19: FINANCIER'S RETURN EXPECTATIONS BY RISK

The Process

As you embark on the process of raising funds, one of your most pressing questions is likely to be: How long will it be until the funds are available? The short answer: It will likely take longer than you think. Most transactions experience delays, often for innocuous reasons. In this section, you will find an outline of investing and lending processes, with estimated time ranges, so you will be well prepared for your fundraising endeavour.

> **INSIDER TIP** ▶ If possible, start the fundraising process early and have enough of a working capital reserve to last you at least twice as long as it generally takes to raise funds (using the outside timeframe). Surprise issues that can cause delays occur often.

Investing

Once an investor has screened the investment opportunity, based on the teaser, presentation and financial model, the investor will pursue a high-level due diligence investigation to better understand the transaction, its risks and its upsides. Assuming the investigation reaches a positive conclusion and is approved by the relevant business unit of the investor, the parties will work towards a letter of intent (LOI) or memorandum of understanding (MOU) outlining the main terms and conditions of an agreement and giving the investor a suitable period of time to perform a detailed due diligence investigation, generally on an exclusive basis. Depending on the type of transaction, this exclusivity period would typically last between 30 and 90 days. This process, from screening the opportunity to execution of an LOI/MOU, may take two to four weeks.

Assuming the detailed due diligence investigation did not unveil any deal breakers, and subject to approval by the investor's investment committee and board, the parties will then enter into negotiation of definitive agreements. At this point, legal due diligence of articles of incorporation, bylaws, ownership titles and encumbrances, representations and warranties, and all material legal agreements will be conducted. The members of the investment committee and the board, if board approval is required, will have been kept informed as the transaction and due diligence investigation progressed, ensuring a smoother approval process when the investment report is submitted for approval. Should the negotiation of definitive agreements lead to material changes that are outside the spirit of the approval the investor obtained from its investment committee/board, another approval from the investment committee/board may be required. Closing of the transaction and movement of funds can be expected within one to three months of the date of the LOI/MOU.

The whole process is bound to take two to six months. If everything moves smoothly, it might be accomplished in less time, but in reality, there are usually obstacles to overcome that delay the process somewhat or materially.

• Meeting/screening • High-level due diligence investigation • Approval by business unit • LOI/MOU drafting, negotiation, execution	2 to 4 weeks
• Detailed due diligence investigation • Approval by investment committee/board • Drafting, negotiation of definitive agreements • Final legal due diligence • Closing and provision of funds	1 to 3 months
Total	**6 weeks to 4 months**

FIGURE 20: ESTIMATED TIMELINE FOR THE INVESTING PROCESS

Lending

First, the account officer will complete the initial screening (based on the borrower's presentation and historical performance, and, in the case of project financing, the project's financial model) and determine whether the lender has an interest in this type of transaction. Subsequently, the account officer will compile some basic information to understand the opportunity better. On that basis, and subject to the business unit's approval, the account officer will provide a discussion paper or non-binding term sheet outlining the main terms and conditions. This process, from opportunity screening to presentation of a non-binding term sheet, typically takes from a few days to two weeks.

Upon negotiation and agreement of the non-binding term sheet, the account officer will complete the detailed due diligence investigation, arrange internally for a credit application to be drafted, and obtain credit approval. Except for very simple transactions, the point person within the credit department will usually have been consulted along the way, as the transaction evolved, to give input on what terms and conditions might be acceptable to the credit committee. The larger and more complex the transaction, the more the credit committee will be consulted beforehand, increasing the probability that the offers in the non-binding term sheet will be approved. That said, the process is not always smooth, and last-minute surprises do frequently crop up during the credit approval process.

Following credit approval, the account manager will provide the borrower with a committed, or binding, term sheet, which the client is asked to accept within a certain period of time. This process, from non-binding term sheet to committed term sheet, will typically take between three weeks and two months. Changes to the committed term sheet or definitive agreements that are in the spirit of the credit approval will not require the account manager to go back to the credit committee. For material changes, however, the account manager will need to seek credit approval.

Once the two parties are aligned, the lender will draft definitive agreements and initiate legal due diligence on items such as articles of incorporation, proper titles of the security, and representations and warranties, culminating in the collateral being established, the definitive agreements being executed and the loan being disbursed. This procedure will take about four weeks.

It should take two to four months from first presentation to disbursement of funds. In some cases, the turnaround may be faster, but I have also experienced several transactions that took much longer.

<ul><li>Meeting/screening</li><li>High-level due diligence investigation</li><li>Approval by business unit</li><li>Non-binding term sheet</li></ul>	A few days to 2 weeks
<ul><li>Detailed due diligence investigation</li><li>Approval by credit committee</li><li>Committed term sheet</li></ul>	3 weeks to 2 months
<ul><li>Drafting, negotiation of definitive agreements</li><li>Final legal due diligence</li><li>Closing and disbursement of funds</li></ul>	4 weeks
Total	**2 to 4 months**

FIGURE 21: ESTIMATED TIMELINE FOR THE LENDING PROCESS

APPENDICES

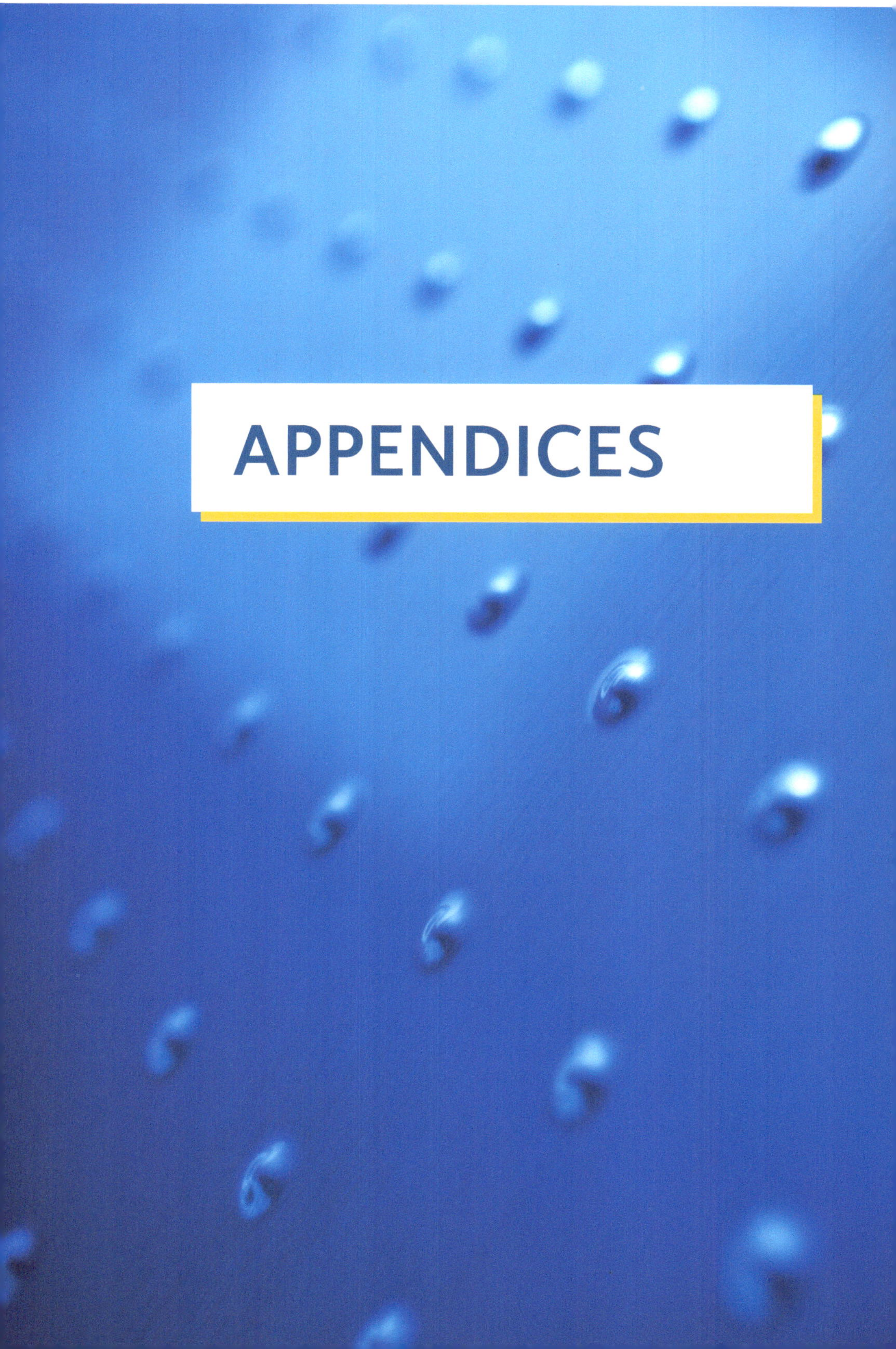

APPENDIX A

Due Diligence Checklist for Prospective Equity Financing

A. Latest Business Plan
1. Who is the company?
2. Corporate history and background
3. Management team, number of employees, organizational chart, corporate organization chart (showing subsidiaries and level of ownership)
4. Competitive landscape and differentiation, barriers to entry (by product lines)
5. Definable technology (intellectual property)
6. Market potential, growth prospects
7. Sales and marketing (process, distribution channels and marketing materials for all product lines, CRM, key people)
8. Customers (nature of main purchases, length of relationship, current business outstanding, revenue size, terms of trade, dependencies/concentration)
9. Regulation
10. Exit strategy

B. Latest Investor Presentation
1. Execution timeline, with the "ask" (amount and type of funds requested) and use of proceeds
2. Previous valuations of the company or its assets
3. Any previous arm's length or other offer for the company or its assets
4. Previous investments, including terms, price and timeline

C. Latest Financial Reports and Model
1. Historical financial performance (last three year-ends; latest interims since year-end, by main profit centres and consolidated)
2. Annual sales mix and gross margins by major product line — historical versus projected
3. Cash flow break-even analysis
4. Financial projections and assumptions (Microsoft Excel)

D. Order Book/Pipeline

E. Share Capitalization Table
1. Copy of the current capitalization table for the company
2. List of all dividends/distributions paid by the company in the past five years
3. List of current officers and directors, including information with respect to the number and class of securities of the company held by each

F. Biographies of Management, Board of Directors, Advisory Board
1. Corporate governance
2. List and bios of individuals (including the term of office for each individual) constituting the current board of directors, officers, committees and board of advisors
3. Minutes of director meetings and meetings of important committees of the board
4. Dependence on key employees

G. State of the Work Environment in Terms of Morale (Turnover) and Health and Safety (Accidents)

H. Conflicts of Interest

Officer, director, employee (or spouse or children of same):

1. Is engaged as a competitor, lessor, lessee, customer or supplier;
2. Owns any assets needed for the business;
3. Owes money to the company; and/or
4. Has an agreement or commitment to receive fees or commissions for services.

I. Contingent Liabilities

1. Ongoing, pending or threatened litigation
2. Other contingent liabilities

J. Suppliers

1. List of major suppliers, terms, percentage of purchase, dependencies
2. Alternative supply services

K. Environmental Problems or Claims

L. Tax

1. Tax returns and notices of (re-)assessment for the last three fiscal years
2. Adequacy of the company's tax provision
3. Loss carry-forwards

M. Insurance

1. Key person insurance
2. Fixed asset insurance
3. Business interruption insurance
4. Commercial general liability insurance
5. Builder's risk insurance/installation floater
6. Other

N. Material Agreements and Documents

1. Articles of incorporation
2. Board of director minutes
3. Supplier contracts
4. Distribution agreements
5. Customer service agreements
6. O&M agreements
7. Licensing agreements
8. Purchase and sale agreements for acquisitions and any related agreements
9. Bank commitment letters
10. Other loan agreements
11. Lease agreements
12. Royalty agreements
13. Employment agreements with management and other key employees (compensation and incentives)
14. Shareholders' agreements
15. Union agreements
16. Pension agreements
17. Stock option agreements
18. Other material agreements

APPENDIX B

Due Diligence Checklist for Prospective Project Financing

SPONSOR

A. Sponsor Company Description
1. Who is the sponsor?
2. Corporate history and background, with focus on development expertise
3. Management team, number of employees, organizational chart, corporate organization chart (showing subsidiaries and level of ownership)
4. Competitive landscape and differentiation, barriers to entry (with respect to project and sponsor company, if different)
5. Latest investor presentation

B. Biographies of Management, Board of Directors, Advisory Board
1. Corporate governance
2. List and bios of individuals (including the term of office for each individual) constituting the current board of directors, officers, committees and board of advisors
3. Minutes of director meetings and meetings of important committees of the board
4. Dependence on key employees

C. State of the Work Environment in Terms of Morale (Turnover) and Health and Safety (Accidents)

D. Financial Performance
1. Historical financial performance (last three year-ends; latest interims since year-end)
2. Tax situation (tax returns and notices of assessment for last three fiscal years)

E. Order Book/Pipeline

F. Financial Projections/Outlook

G. Contingent Liabilities
1. Ongoing, pending or threatened litigation
2. Other contingent liabilities

H. Conflicts of Interest
Officer, director, employee (or spouse or children of same):
1. Is engaged as a competitor, lessor, lessee, customer or supplier;
2. Owns any assets needed for the business;
3. Owes money to the company; and/or
4. Has an agreement or commitment to receive fees or commissions for services.

I. Share Capitalization Tables of Sponsor Company and Project Company
1. Copy of the current capitalization table
2. List of current officers and directors, including information with respect to the number and class of securities held by each

PROJECT

J. Market Potential, Market Research re Project

K. Country Risk (if applicable)

L. Project Company Financials
1. Financial projections and assumptions (Microsoft Excel)
2. The "ask" (sources and uses of total capital expenditure)

M. Project Development Schedule

N. Offtaker(s)
1. Who? Background
2. Report(s) from credit rating agency(ies)

O. Suppliers of Technology and Feedstock
1. Who? Background
2. Report(s) from credit rating agency(ies)

P. Engineering, Procurement and Construction (EPC) Contractor
1. Who? Background
2. Report(s) from credit rating agency(ies)
3. Warranties
4. Insurance
5. Project schedule
6. Payment schedule

Q. Operations and Maintenance ("O&M")
1. Technology (spec sheets, number of generations, operational experience, proven, strengths and weaknesses, third-party engineering report)
2. Feedstock assessment
3. Assumed production
4. O&M provider (Who? Background?)

R. Regulatory Considerations

S. Environmental Problems or Claims

T. Insurance
1. Key person insurance
2. Fixed asset insurance
3. Business interruption insurance
4. Commercial general liability insurance
5. Builder's risk insurance/installation floater
6. Other

U. Material Agreements and Documents

1. Articles of incorporation
2. Board of director minutes
3. Offtake agreement(s)
4. Warranties
5. Supply agreement(s)
6. EPC contract
7. O&M agreement
8. Licensing agreement(s)
9. Royalty agreement(s)
10. Bank commitment letters
11. Other loan agreements
12. Lease agreements
13. Shareholder agreements
14. Employment agreements with management and other key employees (compensation and incentives)
15. Pension agreements
16. Stock option agreements
17. Employee benefits
18. Union agreements
19. Other material agreements

APPENDIX C

Due Diligence Checklist for Prospective Corporate Financing

A. Corporate History/Structure/Ownership
1. Who is the company?
2. Corporate history and background
3. Management team, number of employees, organizational chart, corporate organization chart (showing subsidiaries and level of ownership)
4. Competitive landscape and differentiation, barriers to entry (by product line)
5. Market potential, growth prospects

B. Biographies of Management, Board of Directors, Advisory Board
1. Corporate governance
2. List and bios of individuals (including the term of office for each individual) constituting the current board of directors, officers, committees and board of advisors
3. Minutes of director meetings and meetings of important committees of the board
4. Dependence on key employees

C. Share Capitalization Tables of Sponsor Company and Project Company
1. Copy of the current capitalization table
2. List of current officers and directors, including information with respect to the number and class of securities held by each

D. State of the Work Environment in Terms of Morale (Turnover) and Health and Safety (Accidents)

E. Financial Performance
1. Historical financial performance (last three year-ends; latest interims since year-end, by main profit centres and consolidated)
2. Annual sales mix and gross margins by major product line — historical versus projected
3. Tax situation (tax returns and notices of (re-)assessment for the last three fiscal years)

F. Assets
1. Detailed listing of accounts receivables for the past two fiscal years
2. Information on bad debts for the past two fiscal years
3. Detailed listing of inventories and obsolescence timeline for the past two fiscal years
4. Detailed listing of accounts payable for the past two fiscal years

G. Contingent Liabilities
1. Ongoing, pending or threatened litigation
2. Other contingent liabilities

H. Conflicts of Interest
Officer, director, employee (or spouse or children of same):
1. Is engaged as a competitor, lessor, lessee, customer or supplier;
2. Owns any assets needed for the business;
3. Owes money to the company; and/or
4. Has an agreement or commitment to receive fees or commissions for services.

I. Financial Projections
1. Financial projections and assumptions for the next three years
2. Order book/pipeline

J. Market
1. Competitive landscape and differentiation, barriers to entry (by product line)
2. Market potential, growth prospects

K. Major Customers
Nature of main purchases, length of relationship, current business outstanding, revenue size, terms of trade, dependencies/concentration

L. Sales and Marketing
1. Details of sales distribution channels for product lines
2. Marketing materials for product lines

M. Suppliers
1. List of major suppliers, terms, percentage of purchase, dependencies
2. Alternative supply services

N. Regulatory Considerations

O. Environmental Problems or Claims

P. Insurance
1. Key person insurance
2. Fixed asset insurance
3. Business interruption insurance
4. Commercial general liability insurance
5. Builder's risk insurance/installation floater
6. Other

Q. Management Information System

R. Material Agreements and Documents
1. Articles of incorporation
2. Board of director minutes
3. Supplier contracts
4. Distribution agreements
5. Customer service agreements
6. Licensing agreement(s)
7. Royalty agreement(s)
8. Purchase and sale agreements
9. Bank commitment letters
10. Other loan agreements
11. Lease agreements
12. Shareholders' agreements
13. Employment agreements with management and other key employees (compensation and incentives)
14. Pension agreements
15. Stock option agreements
16. Employee benefits
17. Union agreements
18. Other material agreements

References

Equity Financing

Brealey, Richard, Stewart Myers and Franklin Allen. *Principles of Corporate Finance*, 11th edition. New York: McGraw-Hill: 2013.

Fraser Milner Gasgrain LLP. *Technology Startup Guide, October 5, 2010*. Accessed Sept. 23, 2013. http://www.slideshare.net/fmclaw/tech-startup-guide.

Graves, Brian, Partner, McCarthy Tétrault LLP. *Shareholder Agreements*. Conference presentation, February 21–22, 2005. http://www.mccarthy.ca/pubs/insight_paper_ver_two.pdf.

Koscak, Brian, and David Gilkes. "Compliance with the Accredited Investor Exemption — A Nine-Point Plan for EMDs." Accessed September 23, 2013. http://www.emdacanada.com/?ANinePointPlanfo.

National Venture Capital Association. "Model Legal Documents." Accessed September 23, 2013. http://www.nvca.org/index.php?option=com_content&view=article&id=108&Itemid=136.

Taulli, Tom. "The Perils of a 'Down Round' Financing." *Bloomberg Businessweek*, January 23, 2009. http://www.businessweek.com/printer/articles/32798-the-perils-of-a-down-round-financing.

Toronto Stock Exchange (TSX)/TSX Venture Exchange. http://www.tmx.com.

Walker, Scott Edward. "Beware the Trappings of Liquidation Preference." *VentureBeat*, August 16, 2010. http://venturebeat.com/2010/08/16/beware-the-trappings-of-liquidation-preference/.

World Exchange Federation. http://www.world-exchanges.org/member-exchanges/key-information.

Debt Financing

Brealey, Richard, Stewart Myers and Franklin Allen. *Principles of Corporate Finance*, 11th edition. New York: McGraw-Hill: 2013.

Corrigan, E. Gerald. "Are Banks Special? A Revisitation." *The Region*, March 1, 2000. http://www.minneapolisfed.org/publications_papers/pub_display.cfm?id=3527.

"Deal Analysis: NextEra St. Clair." *ProjectFinance*, November 14, 2012.

Dr. Econ. The Federal Reserve Bank of San Francisco. "What Is the Economic Function of a Bank?" July 2001. http://www.frbsf.org/education/activities/drecon/2001/0107.html.

Grill, Wolfgang, and Hans Perczynski. *Wirtschaftslehre des Kreditwesens*, 45th edition. Cologne: Bildungsverlag EINS, 2011.

Groobey, Chris, John Pierce, Michael Faber and Greg Broome. Wilson Sonsini Goodrich and Rosati Professional Corporation. *Project Finance Primer for Renewable Energy and Clean Tech Projects*. August 2010. http://www.wsgr.com/PDFSearch/ctp_guide.pdf.

Werbeagentur, Marketingberatung, Positionierungsagentur. "Die Goldene Bilanzregel in der Finanzierung." Blog entry by Markus Selders, January 17, 2011. http://blog.beraten-und-umsetzen.de/finanzierung/die-goldene-bilanzregel-in-der-finanzierung/.

Subordinate Financing

CIBC World Markets. *Convertible Bonds Primer*. Last updated July 29, 2004. http://www.cibcwg.com/c/document_library/get_file?uuid=bbb4ddc4-88f9-4373-aa8e-42250e5cb136&groupId=43325&version=1.0.

Odlum Brown Limited. *Convertible Debentures: A Primer*. Accessed September 23, 2013. http://www.inyourbestinterest.ca/uploaded/doc1378.pdf.

Return Calculations

Brealey, Richard, Stewart Myers and Franklin Allen. *Principles of Corporate Finance*, 11th edition. New York: McGraw-Hill: 2013.

Bank for International Settlement (BIS). http://www.bis.org.

Acknowledgements

In the course of writing this book, I have been helped by many wonderful people. First, I would like to thank my friend and business partner Bill Tharp, who not only took the time to review my manuscript and give excellent input, but was also instrumental in drafting the sections on public offerings and value creation.

My editor, Sue Sumeraj, challenged and shaped my writing, and my book designers, Kevin Cockburn and Joseph Gisini, illustrated it pleasingly. Together, they helped turn this book idea of mine into a sophisticated product, for which I am deeply grateful.

I would also like to offer my heartfelt appreciation to Natalie Townsend, who read and critiqued my manuscript, and to Mary-Kathryn Dotzko and Aran Kwinta, who provided valuable input in selected parts of the book.

Many thanks to my mentors and friends from the SuperMind and related programs, particularly Peggy McColl, Gay Hendricks, Mary Morrissey and Bob Proctor, who opened up my mind to writing such a book, and Nancy Thiel Voogd, Sandy Alemian and Gretchen Schoenstein, whose friendship and unconditional love have helped me overcome many a bump in the road.

To proofreader Wendy Potter and indexer Gillian Watts, thank you for the solid work you provided.

Finally, with great appreciation, I would like to thank my wife and best friend, Jean LaMantia, for her love, support and enthusiasm, as well as countless useful comments. Not only did you help improve the manuscript and its title, you also made it so much easier and more enjoyable for me to write this book. And, perhaps most importantly, by writing an essential book yourself, you showed me that I could do so too.

Index

Note: Page numbers in **bold** type indicate the location of definitions.

KATHRIN OHLE, PRINCIPAL AND FOUNDER OF TWIG ENERGY INC. ("TWIG")
TORONTO, ONTARIO, CANADA

In 2009, building on 20 years of experience in investing and lending in the corporate world, Kathrin founded twig, a financial advisory firm that partners with businesses in renewable energy and clean technology. twig provides its clients assistance in 1) raising equity and debt instruments, and 2) purchase and sale of assets, projects and companies. Kathrin is also a senior partner at Tangerine Tango, a like-minded financial advisory firm with a global reach.

Kathrin started her career in corporate banking with Deutsche Bank AG in Germany and Canada, and then, after immigrating to Canada, worked with TD Securities. Subsequently, she was an investment manager for F Capital, a start-up private equity fund; Kensington Capital, a buyout fund; and the Business Development Bank of Canada's subordinate financing fund. Before founding twig, Kathrin was a senior corporate developer at Emera Inc., where she was responsible for expanding the company's asset portfolio through acquisitions or greenfield developments, with a specific focus on renewable energy generation.

During her career, Kathrin has closed bank debt and (quasi) equity transactions of over $5.5 billion, as a corporate lender, financial investor and strategic investor. Alternative energies have been her passion since 2007.

Kathrin has a master's degree in Business Administration from the University of Cologne, Germany.

www.twigenergy.com